STAUNTON HAROLD

John Fox

KAIROS PRESS

Newtown Linford
Leicester
2001

Copyright © John Fox, 2001

ISBN 1-871344-29-8

First Edition, 2001

Layout by Robin Stevenson, Kairos Press
Body text in Century Schoolbook BT 10.5pt
Imagesetting by dotperfect, Leicester
Printed in Great Britain by Norwood Press, Anstey, Leics.

KAIROS PRESS

www.kairos-press.co.uk

552 Bradgate Road
Newtown Linford
Leicester LE6 0HB
Great Britain

TABLE OF CONTENTS.

Foreword by The Rt. Hon. Earl Ferrers P.C. 4

Introduction 5

1. IN THE BEGINNING 9

2. THE CHAPEL 15

3. THE SAINT AND THE SINNER. 23

4. THE HALL 31

5. THE ESTATE 40

6. THE FERRERS FAMILY IN MORE RECENT TIMES 45

7. A FEW TALES AND LEGENDS 53

8. STAUNTON HAROLD AS A CHESHIRE HOME. 57

9. SUE RYDER CARE AT STAUNTON HAROLD. 62

10. ADAPTING TO CHANGE. 64

A Select Bibliography. 70

Index 71

FOREWORD
by The Rt. Hon. Earl Ferrers P.C.

*T*his booklet, in a few pages, covers the history of a family over 900 years and its house.

It is written with style and elegance, and each page compels you to move on to the next. The research and attention to detail has been remarkable, and it records so accurately the different facets of the Shirley family over many centuries.

Recording a family's history can all too easily produce a boring narrative. Not so this book. So well written is it that anyone who starts it will not feel satisfied until he or she comes to the last pages.

It will be a fine addition to the history of the Shirley family and of Staunton Harold, of which the author can be justly proud.

Ferrers
July 2001

INTRODUCTION

Staunton Harold is one of the most beautiful and interesting places in England. But it is also one of England's least known treasures. It is hoped that this little book will help to make visitors to Staunton Harold more aware of the fascinating story of Staunton Harold during the past millennium, of the people who have lived in Staunton Harold Hall during that period and of those who built and worshipped in the Chapel.

In his volume on Leicestershire in the Penguin 'Buildings of England' series, Nikolaus Pevsner said of Staunton Harold: "for position, Staunton Harold, the house and its chapel, are unsurpassed in the country – certainly as far as Englishness is concerned". It is the natural beauty of the place, combined with the mineral wealth to be found under the surface and the obvious advantages of its central position close to the meeting point of three counties, which made Staunton Harold an attractive place in which Saxons and Normans settled. In more recent times, residents in a Cheshire Home for over 30 years and then those in a Sue Ryder Palliative Care Home have appreciated many of the same advantages.

Although it is nearly half a century since the Ferrers family lived at Staunton Harold, members of that family retain a strong interest in their ancestral home, which the author greatly appreciates. The present Earl graciously gave permission for any of his family portraits and other archive materials to be used in this publication.

"The Story of Staunton Harold" was written in 1965 by H.J.Wain and published by the Workers' Educational Association (W.E.A.). Mr Wain's excellent little booklet is unique, for it was written from the perspective of one who was brought up on the Staunton Harold Estate and therefore reflects life on the estate in the early part of the 20th century, when Staunton Harold Hall was still the home of the Ferrers family. Mr Wain's booklet has long been out of print, but his family and the W.E.A. have given their kind permission for some of his material to be used in this book.

Another fascinating glimpse into the past is given in "The Cheshire Home at Staunton Harold", compiled in 1967 by Mrs Drucella Starkey. Some of the material in that booklet has also been used here, particularly *Down Memory Lane*, contributed by the Dowager Countess Ferrers. This is reproduced with the kind permission of the Cheshire Home which is now at Newlands House, Netherseal.

The story of the Staunton Harold estate has been helpfully brought up to date in this volume by the chapter written by Mr John Blunt, whose father bought most of the estate land from Earl Ferrers in 1954. Mr Blunt's memories of Staunton Harold in the second part of the 20th century complement those of Mr Wain in the first half of the century and his work is setting the pattern for it in the future, through the farms and woodland and through the popular Ferrers Craft Centre which he has established in the former stable block.

Especial thanks are due to Mrs Dorothy Watson, who has lived at Staunton for nearly 50 years and who has made available some of the invaluable material which she has collected relating to the Ferrers family and the property before and during that period. Since 1954, when Dorothy and her late husband Stanley purchased the walled gardens at Staunton and set up a garden nursery in them, Mr and Mrs Watson have made a unique contribution to the new community which has developed at Staunton, and through her talks on Staunton Mrs Watson has made many people more aware of the story of the Hall and those who have lived there. Many of the illustrations in this booklet come from Mrs Watson's collection.

One of the joys of being involved with Staunton Harold has always been the friendship and help of the staff and volunteers who are committed to the Hall and to those who live there. Ken Brydson, then Chairman of the House Committee of the Ryder-Cheshire Mission, earned the author's gratitude by initially inviting him to become involved with Staunton Harold. At that time David Arnold, Margaret Duffy, Anne Laws and Julie Langdale made the arrangement of an historic exhibition a pleasure, never a chore. Since then, many of the staff of the Sue Ryder Home – fund-raisers like Julie and Lorraine, Helen and Fiona; Denise, Sally, other members of the nursing staff and Nigel Lees the administrative officer to name but a few – have given a great deal of help and support. John Bowker and Eric Desborough took many of the photographs used in this publication: both have given a great deal of time and effort to Staunton Harold over the years. The author also thanks all the writers and organisations listed in the bibliography, without whose work this book would not have been possible.

Above all, thanks are due to my wife Mary, who has been immensely helpful and patient as I have done the research and compiled this volume about Staunton Harold, a place which has many happy memories for both of us.

But this Introduction has to have a postscript – or perhaps it should be read as a Prologue for the next stage in the life of Staunton Harold. This booklet was being prepared for publication when news came of the impending sale of the Hall by the Ryder-Cheshire Mission and the possible closure of the Sue Ryder Care Home which has been using the premises since 1989. At the time of writing the future is not clear and no-one knows how the Hall will be used in future. But it has served the community well for many generations, it has a special place in the affections and memories of all who have been associated with it, and there is no doubt that whatever purpose it serves in future, those who live and work in it will quickly come to love Staunton Harold as much as those who have been associated with it in the past.

STAUNTON HAROLD HALL
As described by Tom Gair, one of the earliest residents in the Cheshire Home.

Down in the valley, away from all
The bustle and hustle, stands the Hall,
Framed by trees, surrounded by lakes,
A beautiful majestic picture it makes.

As I sit on the lawn, bathed in the sun,
And I see what the wonders of nature have done,
I think what a fortunate person am I,
And heave a deep and grateful sigh.

I remember I came here, not long ago,
Surrounded by people I did not know,.
Yet here I sit, with friends all around,
A more pleasant company I never found.

I listen enraptured to the songs of the birds,
And realise how futile are my words.
The language of humans cannot say
How delightful they sound on such a day.

I look at the lake with its swans and geese,
And waterlilies which seem to increase
With each day, and to me it seems
Nature has exceeded my wildest dreams.

In the middle, and overlooking it all,
Stands the Church, which seems to call
Us all, "Come inside and thank the Lord",
Which we gladly do with one accord.

Whilst I adore these material things,
There's something deeper to which my soul clings,
It's the loving kindness shown to us all
By these God-sent souls inside the Hall.

To most people who come to this place,
It is one of the beauty spots on this country's face,
They take a look, then onward they roam,
But to me it is more, it's become "My Home".

CHAPTER ONE

In the Beginning...

*I*t is not known when the first settlement took place at Staunton Harold. As "STAUNTON" means a stony place, it may seem a strange place in which to establish a community. But as the stone in the ground at Staunton includes sandstone and limestone, coal and iron, copper and lead, the land has been highly valued for many centuries.

After his success at Hastings in 1066, William of Normandy divided England between his followers. One of the most prominent of those supporters was Henry de Ferraris, whose loyalty was rewarded with no less than 210 "lordships". But William knew that if any one Norman had a great concentration of estates, he could develop a power-base and may rival the King himself. Henry's holdings were therefore scattered throughout 14 counties, from Hampshire to Lincolnshire. With 114 of them in Derbyshire and 35 in Leicestershire, his strength was clearly greatest in the East Midlands, but descendants of Henry are to be found throughout England: e.g. Baddesley Clinton, a moated manor house in Warwickshire, is now maintained by the National Trust but was for centuries the home of another branch of the Ferrers family, whose arms are to be seen everywhere: in the church at Baddesley Clinton there is a slab to the memory of twelve generations of Ferrers.

Obviously Henry could neither farm nor supervise all these properties and he had to lease them to feudal underlings. Staunton was "enfeoffed" (leased) to Harold de Lecha, whose ancestors are unknown though he appears to have been a Saxon and his name tells us that he came from that part of Nottinghamshire which is still known as Leake (East

and West). Harold went to live at the manor of Staunton and eventually adopted the name Staunton instead of that of his former place of residence, Leake: Staunton itself becomes known as Staunton Harold to distinguish it from other Stauntons or "Stony Towns", of which there are several in the East Midlands and elsewhere in England.

Around 1105 Robert Ferraris, having inherited the lands of his grandfather Henry, granted land at Shirley in Derbyshire to Fulcher (Shirley), son of Sewalis or Saswalo, who may also have been a Saxon. Arthur Mee said of this family: "The Shirleys have as long a continuous history as any family in England". Saswalo himself held a number of lordships, including Ettington (sometimes spelt Eatington) in Warwickshire, which is still owned by the family: there is a carving in the 19th century Hall at Ettington which reads:

When good St Edward wore the crown
Saswalo here was thane:
His male stem still this manor own
Now in Victoria's reign.

Thus by 1105 there were three great families associated with Staunton Harold, the Ferraris (more recently known as Ferrers) from Normandy and Stauntons/Leakes and Shirleys from Saxon England. It is these three families whose story is constantly interwoven and which together make the family history of Staunton Harold over the last 1000 years.

Throughout the Middle Ages all these families served their King and Country loyally, going on Crusades and achieving many distinctions. Several members of the Ferraris family held the titles of Earl of Derby and Earl of Nottingham, which explains why the family crest is reproduced on John Speede's 1610 map of Nottinghamshire. In 1292 Elias Staunton became the first Knight in the family and Sir Elias served in Parliament as a Knight of the Shire.

The Stauntons endowed many churches and other Christian establishments generously: Robert de Ferraris, with the agreement of the men of Staunton, gave Breedon Church and other land to the Augustinian Priory of St Oswald at Nostell in Yorkshire in 1144, on condition that the Priory would find at their own cost a chaplain to minister at Staunton every day except St Hardulph's day (now observed on 21st August). This probably maintained an older arrangement, as the Church of St Mary and St Hardulph at Breedon is believed to have originated in Saxon times. It was a Minster, from which priests would go and minister to the needs of communities in the vicinity, including Staunton. Breedon Church is the only Church dedicated to St Hardulph.

It is not certain who St Hardulph was, but he may have lived in a cell or cave in a cliff near the river Trent, perhaps in the "anchor" church near Ingleby. He is said to have taken books about the saints to a holy woman named Modwen (to whom the parish church at Burton on Trent is dedicated) and two women were saved from drowning when they were trying to obtain a book which Hardulph had forgotten to take to Modwen. But there is also a suggestion that a King with a similar name may have been buried at Breedon in Saxon times, as in The Chronicle of Hugh Candidus there is a reference to the burial at Breedon of *"sanctus Aerdulfus rex"* ("the holy King Hardulph"). Two kings with the name of Hardulph are recorded in Saxon times, one in Northumbria c.800A.D. and the other in Kent, but there is nothing to link either of them or three Bishops of the same name with Breedon. Ann Dornier in her "Mercian Studies" concludes that "one has to consider the possibility that St Hardulf was adopted in the early medieval period at Breedon because of Hugh Candidus' statement and that there is no historical basis for the dedication". The additional dedication to

St. Hardulph's Church, Breedon on the Hill, when parts of the ruined priory were still there. (from Nichols, 1804)

St Mary was probably added by the Normans, who did not always recognise the validity of Celtic or Saxon saints!

Sir Thomas Shirley, who died in 1362, is described as "the great father of the family of Shirley". It was he who endowed the Collegiate Church of St Mary in the Newarke in Leicester, which had been founded in 1354 by Henry Duke of Lancaster. For the next two centuries members of the Shirley family were buried in this church, of which only fragments now survive.

Sir Thomas married well, and his wife Isabel Drayton brought more wealth to the Shirleys in the form of land. Hugh Shirley became Grand Falconer in Ireland to King Henry IV and was one of the knights so close to the King that he wore the King's armour in battle to deceive the enemy: he was killed at the battle of Shrewsbury in 1403, but he is remembered as "valiant Shirley" in Shakespeare's Henry IV Part I, where the custom of being disguised as the King leads to the line: "Another king! They grow like Hydra's heads". Ralph Shirley was one of Henry V's leading commanders at Agincourt and Harfleur in 1415 and was buried in the church in Leicester. A later Ralph fought for King Henry VII at the final battle of the Wars of the Roses, at East Stoke in Nottinghamshire in 1487, and was made a banneret on the battlefield i.e. he was given what today might be called a field commission and knighted on the battlefield for bravery on that particular occasion.

Neither Stauntons nor Shirleys received an hereditary peerage during this long period. But they were highly regarded and there are manuscripts in the British Museum Library, quoted by Nichols in his great History of Leicestershire, which record from 1609 "7 Remarkable Principles so Rare, so Eminent and Singular that they are found in few other families". Those Principles are set out in great detail in the manuscripts but may be summarised as:

Chartley Castle, Staffordshire. Built in the 13th century, Mary, Queen of Scots, was held prisoner there in 1585. It passed by marriage to the Shirley family, who later sold it to pay for refurbishment at Staunton. Chartley was burnt down in 1791.

1. *Nobleness and antiquity of blood.*
2. *Contracted alliances with the ancient and most illustrious houses of England.*
3. *Prowess, memorable acts and high attempts, fortitude and glorious military virtue.*
4. *Great devotion and singular fidelity to sovereign princes.*
5. *Bright and renowned alliances to royal stems.*
6. *Great lands and seignories held from antiquity have given no small addition of honour to the name.*
7. *Holy Piety – they have religiously maintained. Also ardent and inextinguishable charity.*

Clearly these Principles record the history of a very remarkable family – even if there is a small element of wishful thinking about one or two of them: for example, there had been no marriages into the royal family before 1609, but there was one soon after, as in the 1620's, Henry Shirley married Dorothy, daughter of Robert Devereux, Earl of Essex and Eu, Lord Ferrers of Chartley and a descendant of Thomas Duke of Gloucester, son of King Edward III.

The marriage alliances which had taken place had not only brought the family great distinction and wealth; they had also brought together the Stauntons and the Shirleys. In 1423 Margaret Staunton was the heir of the Staunton estates and married Ralph Shirley. Both Shirleys and Stauntons had married into the Meignell family of Langley Meignell in Derbyshire and Margaret and Ralph were therefore distant cousins. As a consequence of their relationship "within the fourth degree of consanguinity", dispensation for the marriage had to be obtained from Pope Martin V, not least to ensure that Margaret was not being stolen away or forced into the marriage. The Papal dispensation was forthcoming and henceforth the family name of the lords of Staunton Harold is Shirley.

It was the son of Ralph and Margaret, John Shirley, who transferred his seat, his principal home, to Staunton Harold "where his successors have ever since flourished", as Nichols put it.

The 1597 tomb at Breedon of George Shirley and his wife with lifelike carvings of the family group above and an unnerving alabaster carved skeleton at the base.

Staunton Harold is in the parish of Breedon on the Hill. It had long been the practice for services to be held at Staunton Harold on any day except St Hardulph's day, when all parishioners were expected to worship in the parish church dedicated to St Hardulph. But when King Henry VIII dissolved the monasteries, Augustinian establishments like Breedon Priory were also closed and sold. Francis Shirley bought Breedon so that henceforth the Shirleys had the right to be buried there. The family pew (1627) may be seen in Breedon Church: it is described in the "History Guide" to Breedon Church as a "monstrous item of privacy-seeking furniture" which originally stood in the body of the nave. The north aisle was taken over by the Shirleys as a family mausoleum. The family tombs date back to Francis Shirley and his wife (1571). The greatest tomb is that of George Shirley and his wife, with two babies in cradles and two sons and a daughter behind: this is what is sometimes described as a "transit" tomb, for in double-decker form it shows the family in life-like dress and appearance at the top, and reduced to skeletons below, thus symbolising the fate that befalls all mortals.

Right: The present Earl Ferrers and his younger son looking at the family pedigree.

At long last the opportunity for an hereditary title arose. King James VI of Scotland had become James I of England and decided to settle Protestant Scots in Catholic Ireland. The Irish did not take kindly to this "Plantation of Ulster", as it was known, and so soldiers were needed to protect the Scottish Protestants in Ulster. Soldiers cost money and it was therefore suggested to James I by Sir Thomas Shirley, a distant relation of the Shirleys of Staunton Harold from Wiston in Sussex, that a new hereditary order should be created. This new order of Baronets would rank between Barons and Knights: like the latter, the

gentlemen would carry the title of Sir and their wives would be known as Lady, but unlike knights, their sons would inherit the Baronetcy. In order to have a Baronetcy, gentlemen were required to provide 30 footsoldiers and to maintain them in Ireland for 3 years: but most of the new Baronets chose to make a cash payment to the King instead, the amount being £1,095 i.e. the total cost of maintaining 30 soldiers at 8d per day for 3 years: at the former *Lsd* rate of 240d to the pound, 30 soldiers @ 8d (about 3.5p) per day cost exactly £1 per day, £1,095 for the 1,095 days in 3 years. Thus for £1,095, on 22nd May 1611 George Shirley was the 4th gentleman on the earliest list of the creation of Baronets and became Sir George Shirley.

Sir George now knew that his line would continue to be Baronets. But he did not want it to be thought that the line had begun with him in 1611. He therefore commissioned a family tree to record the achievements of the Shirleys and all the families associated with them. In 1627 what is normally known as the Lesser Pedigree was produced: though known as "lesser" pedigree, it measures 13 feet 10 inches by 6 feet! The only reason for calling this the Lesser Pedigree is that in 1632 the definitive Great Pedigree was produced, measuring 30 feet by 13 feet.

Sir George's son Henry, who was to become the second Baronet, is said to have been mainly responsible for the production of this wonderfully informative and ornate document, which is now kept in Leicestershire County Archives. This Pedigree shows in great detail not only all the births and deaths in the family, but it also records the achievements of the various members of the family, their marriages and other details about them. It is illuminated with colourful pictures of the family in appropriate garments at different times: tombs and memorial brasses are illustrated, as are family crests recording different alliances. The "Stemmata Shirleiana" has been described as "one of the earliest family histories written in a spirit of critical enquiry". It is a tremendous work of historical research and art – but it is so large that it is brought out only on very rare occasions, such as the gathering of members of the Shirley family from all over the world. There was nowhere at Staunton Harold where this could be displayed in recent times and this priceless document was kept rolled up on the floor in the dining room: if the children of the family wanted to look at it, they took it out onto the tennis court, as it was too big to be unrolled anywhere else.

By 1632 the Shirley family had a home, a church, an hereditary title and a proud past which had been fully recorded. What would the next 350 years bring?

CHAPTER TWO

THE CHAPEL

*S*everal baronets followed George in rapid succession. Henry was the second: he had married Dorothy Devereux, daughter of Robert Earl of Essex who had been the great favourite of Queen Elizabeth I: the Earl of Essex owned the estate and castle at Chartley in Staffordshire. Sir Henry is said to have "cared for no Lord in England but the Lord of Hosts" – perhaps an indication of the attitude of his family which led to the building of the Chapel. Sir Henry was quickly succeeded by Sir Charles who was "a considerable sufferer by the civil war" and had to pay £600 by order of Parliament in order to preserve his property from confiscation. Those were very difficult times. The Civil War began in 1642 and the Shirleys found themselves in the thick of it. The Shirleys had remained Roman Catholics after the Reformation and Sir Henry was attended on his deathbed by a Catholic priest. But Sir Henry's wife was an Anglican and her children were brought up as high church Anglicans and staunch supporters of the monarchy. When Parliament led by Oliver Cromwell won the war and the King was imprisoned and eventually executed, Royalists like the Shirleys were very vulnerable.

Robert Shirley had succeeded his brother Charles and become the 4th Baronet in 1642. Sir Robert was an "early and zealous advocate for the cause of his royal master". He had been a friend at Oxford of William Laud, who became Archbishop of Canterbury and was executed by order of Parliament in 1645. Several leading churchmen who were out of sympathy with the Puritan government were given asylum at Staunton Harold, including future Archbishops of Canterbury and York

Sir Robert is believed to have been one of the leaders of the Sealed Knot, a resistance movement which continued to harass Cromwell's regime. Staunton Harold was in an area where there were several great families which strongly supported the Royalist cause, notably the Harpurs at Calke Abbey, the Hastings at Castle Donington and the Shirleys

Sir Robert Shirley, 4th Baronet, a zealous Royalist who may have fought for the restoration of the Monarchy, even during Cromwell's regime. (Picture from Nichol's History of Leicestershire)

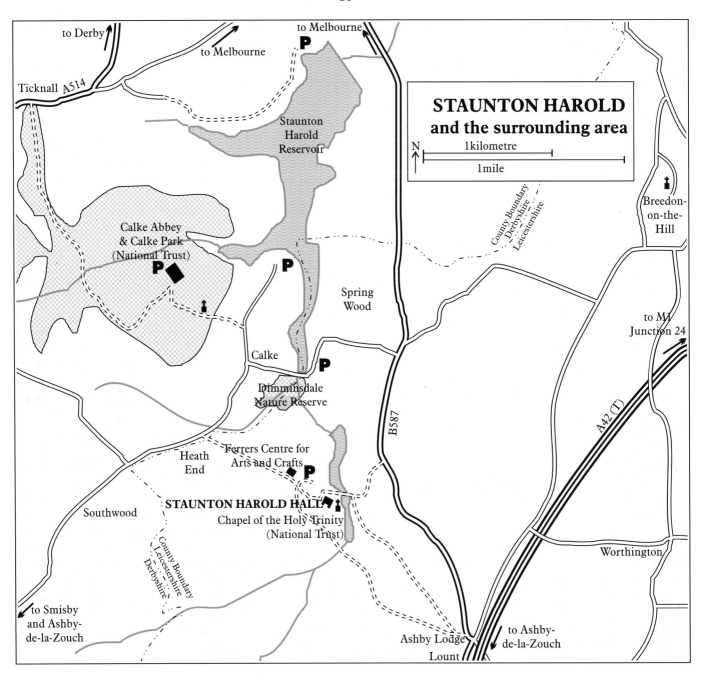

themselves. Robert was arrested and imprisoned on several occasions: in 1648 a dispute with the Parliamentarian garrison in Ashby de la Zouch led to him being charged with having 100 muskets and 25 cases of pistols hidden in a coalpit. He was taken to Leicester prison but released on that occasion. In 1652 he was accused of saying that "he would not suffer any that acted for Parliament to live upon his lands". His final arrest on 5th May 1654 on a warrant issued by the Council of State "to seize, inventory and secure all his estates" led to his imprisonment in the Tower of London. His servant William Drinkwater was admitted to the Tower to help him but, although nothing was ever proved against Sir Robert, he died in the Tower on 6th November 1656, "not without suspicion of poison". There is a portrait of Sir Robert which is attributed to Van Dyck.

Sir Robert served his King well but will always be better remembered for the way in which he served his God. It is said that he was "the first of his family to adhere to the Anglican faith with conviction". It was Sir Robert who ordered the building of the marvellous chapel at Staunton Harold. An Order in Council said of him: "He that could afford to build a church could no doubt afford to equip a ship" – but of course Sir Robert would not supply a ship for the navy of the Commonwealth.

A room in the house had probably served as a chapel before his time: it is believed that the room which became the chapel of the Sue Ryder Home had been used by Sir Henry as a Roman Catholic chapel. But it was Sir Robert who built the unique family chapel which is one of very few chapels/churches built anywhere in England during the Commonwealth period, the others being at Berwick on Tweed (1645), Brampton Bryan in Herefordshire and St Wilfred's Chapel at Brougham in Westmoreland (1656-60). The chapel at Staunton Harold is unique because it

remains almost exactly as it was designed nearly 350 years ago. It is a fine example of High Church architecture and it is unusually faithful to medieval traditions of church architecture. In the programme for the tercentenary celebrations of the chapel in 1953 it was described as "the only one in England completely planned, built and equipped during the period of the Commonwealth when the building of churches was forbidden." Clearly Sir Robert built it as an affront to the Puritan government of which he did not approve.

Sir Robert was conscious that he might not survive to see his Chapel completed. In his Will dated November 1654 he wrote: "In case the church that I am now building at Staunton Harold … shall not be finished and perfected before my decease, then I doe give and bequeath so much money as my executor shall think convenient to finish and perfect the same, according to my intention". At Sir Robert's funeral service Rev. Gilbert Sheldon preached on the text from Luke VII verse 5: "He loved our country and has built us a synagogue".

Completed in 1653, the chapel at Staunton Harold is built on the traditional east/west axis so that the worshippers facing the altar at the east end are also facing Jerusalem. This means that the chapel is at an unusual angle to the Hall, which was redesigned about 100 years later to have its main entrance near the chapel. The weathered sandstone of the church, the red brick of the Hall and the lawn running down to the lake combine to make an unforgettable impression on everyone who sees them. The Chapel of the Holy Trinity at Staunton Harold is now in the care of the National Trust, which has produced a small handbook about it. The Trust has worked steadily to restore the church, which is open for services and visitors. It is, surprisingly, the only building owned by the National Trust in Leicestershire.

Earl Ferrers' Chapel of the Holy Trinity, built by Sir Robert Shirley in 1653, and now in the care of the National Trust.

The most striking fact about the chapel is that it was built at all. It was also designed with loving care and no expense was spared in its construction and fittings. Sir Robert made no secret of his joy in building the Chapel: indeed, around the south, east and west walls of the chancel, at the top of the wall, runs the inscription in bold capitals:

"SIR ROBERT SHIRLEY BARONET
FOUNDER OF THIS CHURCH:
ANNO DOMINI 1653
ON WHOSE SOUL GOD HATH
MERCY".

The architecture of the Chapel is not unusual. Indeed, Pevsner said of it: "Staunton Harold church was not intended to be a show piece, and that makes it all the more loveable". Though similar in style to many other English churches, it is a notable example of the very late Gothic style of architecture, "built almost two centuries after this style had ceased to be fashionable" (Wain). There are masons' marks on some of the stones but the name of the original architect /master builder is not known, which is not surprising as he may have wished to remain anonymous in those dangerous times. There must have been one designer: as Louis Osman wrote: "There is an overall unity of structure, proportion and colour which reflects one single mind with a clear objective and which rules out the idea of a number of individual local craftsmen working to old-fashioned rules". No doubt Sir Robert took advice from the best architects of his day. The construction work appears to have been completed in 1662/5 by "Richard Shepheard Artifex" [i.e. an artificer, a skilled craftsman] who carved his name and profession on the back of the parapet of the chancel.

It is the interior of the chapel which is truly remarkable. It is the "amazing completeness" of the furnishings and fittings which delighted Pevsner. The interior of the chapel remains virtually unchanged from the time of its building – even the woodwork, known to have been the work of William Smith, who made the pulpit and lectern, the box-pews and the panelling and the great screen which supports the organ loft. The wooden ceiling has a painting of the Creation signed by Zachary and Samuel Kyrk and dated 1655. It appears that the Kyrks painted only the nave ceiling, for a Mr Lovett was paid £26 in 1662 for "clowding the iles" and also £25 for "clouding the Chancell", according to the account book of Sir Seymour Shirley.

Above William Smith's screen there is an organ of which the origins are not known, though it may be the work of "Father" Smith or one of his nephews (not the same family as the joiners Smith). It is believed that the

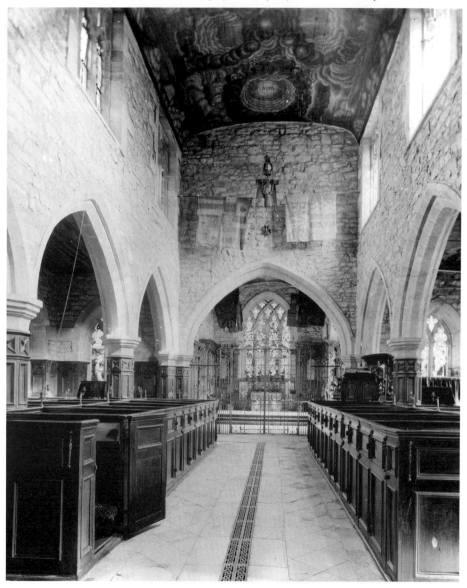

The interior of Staunton Harold chapel, as it looked in 1913. The biggest change since then has been the rendering and whitewashing of the walls.
Picture courtesy of Country Life Picture Library.

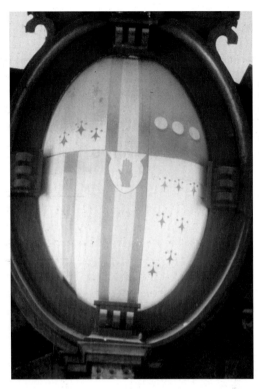

The Shirley family crest above the organ.
The Red Hand of Ulster in the centre is a reminder that the bearer contributed to the Plantation of Ulster.

Several restorations have not changed the pipework of the organ at Staunton Harold and the instrument is of great interest to musicians and organists. "On this little organ at Staunton Harold, with its fresh, vigorous attack and pure quality of sound, can be recreated the great compositions of the 16th and 17th century composers as they intended them to be heard". (Osman).

But also of great interest is the family crest at the top of the organ case. In the centre of this crest is a red hand – the red hand of Ulster. Because of the origins of the order of Baronets in the Plantation of Ulster in 1611, every baronet has a red hand in his crest. The origin of this symbol lies in the story of two chieftains who were being rowed in separate boats towards the shore of Ulster. They had agreed that the one who touched the shore first could claim the land as his kingdom. O'Neill, the chieftain whose boat was losing the race, took a sword, cut off his left hand and threw it ashore so that he could claim Ulster for himself and his successors. That is said to be how the family of O'Neills came to rule Ulster and why they took an open and upright bleeding hand as their family symbol, which may still be seen on postage stamps and throughout Ulster today.

All the fittings in the chapel are worthy of special note, not least because most of them were made at the same time as the Chapel was being built. The purple velvet draperies of the altar frontal and of the pulpit are said to have been made from Archbishop Laud's own vestments and embroidered in silver and gold by the nuns of the Little Gidding community in Cambridgeshire. The wrought-iron screen was made by Robert Bakewell of Derby, a very well known blacksmith who also made the screen for Derby cathedral and the arbour at nearby Melbourne Hall. The box pews are not only contemporary with the building – they continue in use as they were in the 17th

organ may have been designed for use in the Hall before the Chapel was built, but the false front carries the date 1686, which may indicate that the organ was moved into the chapel at that date and given a front designed to look right in the Chapel. It is not surprising that the organ was not put into the Chapel in the 1650s: in 1644 a Lords and Commons Ordnance had ordered the "speedy demolishing of all organs … throughout the kingdom … the better to accomplish the blessed reformation so happily begun and to remove offences and things illegal in the worship of God". It has been suggested that the installation of the organ in the Chapel at Staunton Harold soon after the Restoration of the monarchy in 1660 was the start of a new era of organ repair and building in England.

century, for the custom is still observed of men sitting on the south side of the central aisle with ladies on the north side. Sir Robert and his Lady Katherine and their sons Seymour, Sewallus and Robert would feel very much at home in the chapel as it is today, for it remains just as they designed it.

The chapel also includes some reminders of the Shirley family's earlier activities. There are funerary banners and armour, and a Saracen's head as a reminder of their involvement in the Crusades. As recently as 1956, according to Osman, there were "three sets of funerary achievements with crest, helmet, mantling, surcoat, shield, sword, gauntlet and banners which form such a decorative feature and so appropriately link with the antiquarian and heraldic interests of 'Sir Robert the good' and his uncle Sir Thomas. There is a magnificent Greenwich gauntlet of the Henry VIII period, (beautifully restored by the Tower armouries) and a gold damascened helmet". Unfortunately most of these items have been lost in recent years.

But the magnificent silver-gilt altar silver has not been lost, though it is no longer at Staunton Harold. In 1954 the 12th Earl Ferrers gave the chapel to the National Trust and the altar silver

The altar silver made for the chapel at Staunton Harold is a remarkable collection of 17th century Gothic revival plate. It is now in the care of the Victoria & Albert Museum, London.

was subsequently deposited in the Victoria and Albert Museum in London for safe-keeping. Some of it has been lent by the V&A to Leicester's New Walk Museum, where it can be more readily viewed by people in the East Midlands. All of the silver is contemporary with the chapel itself and is of the highest quality, probably having been designed by Laud's own silversmith. The chalice for the communion wine and the paten for the bread date from 1640/41 and are described as "a fine example of the Gothic revival plate of the 17th century made under the influence of William Laud and the High Church Party". The candle-sticks are by the same maker as a pair now in Rochester Cathedral, and these two pairs are the oldest known to exist in England today. The communion chalices and alms dish are all equally special. Sir Robert spared no expense in ensuring that his chapel had the best of everything.

The diagonal clock in the tower is not quite contemporary with the chapel, as it was not installed until 1716. But like everything else in the Chapel, it has remained unspoilt and is of great interest to horologists.

The only tomb in the chapel of any significance is that of Robert Shirley, great-grandson of Sir Robert the builder. This Robert died of smallpox when he was 21 in 1714. Most of the family, including Sir Robert and his wife, are buried in a vault beneath the chapel. There is a mausoleum in the grounds on the south side of the chapel where the 10th Earl and his Countess are buried.

Sir Robert is never to be forgotten in the chapel at Staunton Harold. In 1953 it was said: "The badge of courage and conviction of this Anglican and Royalist Shirley was the building of Staunton Harold Church". Above the great west door is an ornate sculpture with a coat-of-arms and an epitaph to Sir Robert which was written by Archbishop Gilbert Sheldon of Canterbury, one of the divines who had been given sanctuary in the Hall during the Civil War. The inscription reads:

In the yeare 1653
when all thinges Sacred were throughout ye nation
Either demollisht or profaned
Sᴿ Robert Shirley Barronet
Founded this church
Whose singular praise it is
to haue done the best things in ye worst times
And
hoped them in the most callamitous
The Righteous shall be had in euerlasting
remembrance

Sadly, the Chapel at Staunton Harold, like most of the property, fell into a state of disrepair during the Second World War. An appeal was launched in "The Times" in 1953 by the then Archbishop of Canterbury and the Pilgrim Trust to raise the funds necessary to repair it. On 26th September 1953 the chapel celebrated its tercentenary with a special Laudian service conducted by the Archbishop of Canterbury, Dr Geoffrey Fisher: a talk was given later on the architecture and furnishings of the chapel by John Betjeman and there was also a recital of appropriate 17th century music, mainly on the organ. In his address, Dr Fisher spoke of the significance of the chapel's foundation during the Commonwealth period, when it was built as an expression of living courage and hope. He said that the foundation and adornment of the building in the manner and after the beliefs of Archbishop Laud revealed the courage and confident hope that the Anglican faith would be restored and enduring.

It may have been noted that reference has been made only to the CHAPEL at Staunton Harold and never to the building as a Church. This lovely building was erected to the Glory of God and as a private chapel for use by the Shirley family and others who live on the estate at Staunton Harold. It has never been a parish church and it is not licensed for weddings and funerals, for which a Special Licence has to be obtained from the Archbishop's Registry. It is therefore properly known as a Chapel and not as a church and its full name is *Earl Ferrers' Chapel of the Holy Trinity.*

CHAPTER THREE

THE SAINT AND THE SINNER

Sir Robert was dead. His family was in very great danger. At the very least they might lose all their possessions, even if they did not lose their lives. Any contact between them and the royal family whom Robert had served so loyally could be disastrous. This explains why Charles, later King Charles II, did not write to Sir Robert's widow Katherine Lady Shirley until 20th October 1657. Even then his letter, in his own handwriting, was most discreetly written in guarded language and hidden in the flyleaf of a Bible. Written from "Brusselles", the letter says:

> "It hath been my particular care of you that I have this long deferred to lament with you the great losse that you and I have sustained, least insteede of comforting, I might further expose you to the will of those who will be glad of any occasion to do you further prejudice, but I am promised that this shall be put safely in your hands, though it may not be so soone as I wish; and I am very willing that you should know w(hi)ch I suppose you cannot doute that I beare a greate parte with you of your affliction, and whenever it shall be in my power to make it lighter, you shall see I retayne a very kinde memory of your frinde *[Charles was too canny to put her at risk by referring to her "husband"]* by the care I shall have of you and all his relations, and on this you may depende upon the worde of
> Your very affectionate frinde
> CHARLES R."

This royal promise, made in extremely difficult circumstances, was kept when the monarchy was restored and Charles became King Charles II in 1660.

Their estates were restored to the Shirleys. In 1677 Robert, the son of the earlier Sir Robert, was given the title of Baron Ferrers of Chartley, a title which had become extinct but to which the family had some claim through the second Baronet's marriage to Dorothy Devereux. Baron Ferrers was a lover of fine books and an early Fellow of the Royal Society. He was a Privy Counsellor to William III and Queen Anne. In 1711 Queen Anne raised Lord Ferrers even higher by giving him the titles of Earl Ferrers and Viscount Tamworth. It is small wonder that the Bible in which Charles II made his promise is the one item which the present Earl has reclaimed from Leicestershire County Archives, where it had been deposited by his father with other family papers.

Lord Ferrers was very close to Charles II and his Court. He was Master of the Horse and Steward of the Household of the Queen, Catharine (of Braganza). But he also lived up to his new status and it was said of him that he "keeps a hospitable house and entertains nobly". He began to rebuild Staunton Harold on a Palladian plan, laying out formal gardens and "water-works" to set off his new library front: he also had the grand staircase installed, with its rich ironwork.

The first Earl Ferrers married Elizabeth daughter of Laurence Washington of Wiltshire, the family which later produced the first President of the United States of America. Elizabeth gave Ferrers 10 sons and 7 daughters, many of whom died in infancy or childhood. When Elizabeth herself died Lord Ferrers married again and his second wife, Selina Finch, gave him 5 more sons and 5 more daughters.

It has already been noted that there is a family mausoleum near the Chapel at Staunton Harold. But there is another resting-place for members of the Shirley family, at Ettington in Warwickshire. The ancient Parish Church at Ettington is now in ruins, but part of it was restored in 1825 and converted into a Shirley mortuary chapel, with monuments dating back to the 15th century. The most interesting memorial at Ettington is in memory of the 1st Earl Ferrers and his

The grand staircase with its rich ironwork was built as part of a major redesign of Staunton Harold by the 1st Earl Ferrers.

second wife Selina (nee Finch). The Earl left some money to one of the sons of his second marriage, George, for the erection of a monument, which George finally commissioned almost 60 years later, around 1775 from a respected London sculptor, John Francis Moore. The monument was executed in accordance with contemporary style and is a good example of Moore's love of coloured marbles, with cold white contrasting with grey or black. But the dominant figure is George himself, flanked by his parents. Sir Robert's grandson, Washington Shirley, by then the 5th Earl Ferrers and head of the family in residence at Staunton Harold, refused to permit it to be erected in the Chapel at Staunton Harold. This interesting reminder of that family dispute is commemorated in two inscriptions on the tomb:

Compliance to the Will
of the Right Hon. Robert Earl Ferrers
His Son the Hon. George Shirley
By his second Wife
Who is represented by the above Figure
Has erected this Monument.

The Monument to the Memory
of Robert Earl Ferrers and his Countess Selina
as intended and prepared to be erected in the Church
at Stanton(sic) Harold in the County of Leicester
where he was buried.
By the consent of WASHINGTON Earl FERRERS
But (after being finished)
was refused to be Placed There.
It is erected in this Church at the Expence
of the Honble. George Shirley,
the CENTRE FIGURE in the Monument.

When the 1st Earl died in 1717 he was succeeded by his second son, Washington, who married the daughter of an Irish judge. (Several members of the family married into Irish society). One of Washington's daughters was Selina, who became a very devout Christian when she was still very young. Selina married Theophilus Hastings, 9th Earl of Huntingdon, who lived quite close to Staunton Harold, at Donington Hall.

The Hastings, who had been given the title of Earl of Huntingdon by King Henry VIII in 1529, descended from the Plantagenets and therefore could claim a royal lineage. They had lived at Ashby de la Zouch Castle, but this was demolished in 1648 on Cromwell's orders and they then moved to Donington. Her husband was sympathetic to Selina's spiritual interests, even when she became intimate with John and Charles Wesley, who were embarking on their evangelical revival. In 1739 Selina became a member of the first "Methodist" society and in 1744 she entertained those attending the first Methodist Conference in her London home, at 12 Downing Street, which is now the Government Whips' office.

When the Earl of Huntingdon died in 1746 the Countess was even more free to follow her own desires and to devote her time and her considerable fortune to supporting the Christian revival movement. Selina supported itinerant lay preachers and had George Whitefield and other evangelical preachers in her home as her chaplains – a far cry from the meek and subservient Anglican chaplains to whom the aristocracy were then accustomed. Selina undertook many good works: she rebuked the Archbishop of Canterbury for holding social gatherings of questionable taste at Lambeth Palace, she persuaded David Garrick to drop a play in which Whitefield was ridiculed, and she obtained redress for persecuted Methodists who were not protected from mobs by

Selina, daughter of the 2nd Earl Ferrers, who married Theophilus Hastings, 9th Earl of Huntingdon. She worked tirelessly in support of the 18th century Christian revival. There are still churches belonging to the Countess of Huntingdon's connexion.

have in his hand a note he had just written to the Countess asking her to remember him in her prayers.

Selina fell out with the Wesley brothers when she adopted the Calvinistic belief in the Salvation of a select few, whereas the Wesleys believed in the Salvation of all believers. Selina established a training college for preachers at Trevecca in Wales and financed the building of 67 chapels in many parts of Britain, the first of which was opened in Brighton in 1761. About 25 of these still exist today, together with a considerable number of churches and schools in Sierra Leone. In Britain The Countess of Huntingdon's Connexion is one of the churches in membership of the Free Church Council.

Selina Countess of Huntingdon died on 17th June 1791. She was a remarkable woman who won the respect of all who knew her. To Horace Walpole she was the "Queen of Methodists". To George Whitefield she was "That Elect Lady, that Mother in Israel". In any generation Selina Countess of Huntingdon would have stood out as a shining example of a great Christian. In her own time, she was a spiritual phenomenon.

Selina was not the only significant Christian in the family in the 18th century. Her cousin Walter was ordained in the Anglican church but was a revivalist preacher, like the Wesleys. He was very close to Selina and wrote hymns for her, some of which survived in the Methodist Hymnbook until very recently. Selina's husband's godson, Theophilus Henry Hastings, became Vicar of East and West Leake, and thus took the family back to the roots from which Harold had brought it 700 years earlier.

But there was a black sheep in the family too. In August 1745, Laurence inherited the title and became the 4th Earl Ferrers. It is suggested that Laurence may have been mentally unstable. Certainly his life suggests that he easily lost control of himself and his

magistrates. She won the high opinion of King George III, who said that he wished he had a Lady Huntingdon in every diocese in his Kingdom. It is said that when one of the ladies at Court explained the Countess's repeated absence from Court by sneeringly saying: "I suppose she is busy praying with her beggars", the Prince of Wales responded: "When I am dying, I think I shall be happy to seize the skirt of Lady Huntingdon's mantle to lift me up with her to Heaven."

Selina was a remarkable woman who was greatly revered in her own time. Dr John Potter, the Archbishop of Canterbury who had ordained John Wesley, collapsed and died in 1747 – and was found to temper. He is said to have kicked a groom so brutally that the man died some time later, allegedly as a result of this ill-treatment. Different in every way from Selina, Laurence was excommunicated by the Church of England.

Laurence had had a mistress, Margaret Clifford, since about 1743, and they had four daughters: Margaret lived at Staunton Harold and acted as Housekeeper. The Earl married Mary Meredith in 1752, but there was little or no joy in the marriage: Laurence was often drunk, he beat Mary and threatened to kill her, and she was often ill. His marriage ended when a separation was agreed: this had to be by Act of Parliament, as he was a Peer of the Realm, and it was very unusual if not unique in the 18th century. The Act said that the estate should be vested in Trustees and that John Johnson, who had been Land Steward to Laurence's father as well as to Laurence, should receive the rents and make the necessary payments from them.

On 18th January 1760 there was a dispute between the Earl and Johnson and the Earl shot Johnson. At first the wound did not seem to be fatal – Johnson walked upstairs to his bedroom. Dr Thomas Kirkland from Ashby de la Zouch was called and he later wrote a long narrative in which he recorded all the details of the incident. The Earl talked about Johnson being a villain, gave his reasons for shooting him and discussed the possibility that he might die, with the consequence that "they take off my head", and life proceeded almost normally in the Hall, with supper being served for the doctor and the Earl in the room where Mr Johnson was shot, "a very fine cold Turkey & Brawn" which Dr Kirkland could not enjoy in the circumstances. Dr Kirkland thought that the wound would prove fatal, as the bullet was lodged inside Mr Johnson, so he recruited 7 or 8 colliers to apprehend the Earl, and he also loaded two guns.

Laurence, 4th Earl Ferrers.

Mr Johnson did indeed die at about 9.00 next morning, in his own home, to which he had been taken with some difficulty. Those present were incensed and chased the Earl, firing at him, but he got into the Hall and shut the door. He eventually surrendered to one of the colliers some 6 or 7 hours later, although the Earl

A portrayal of the scene at Tyburn when the Earl was hanged in public on 5th May 1760.

had with him "a double-barrelled gun besides several pistols loaded and a dagger". Several more loaded guns and pistols were found in the house.

The Earl was taken to the White Hart at Ashby. After a Coroner's Jury had returned a verdict of wilful murder, the Earl was taken to Leicester, where his jailer was the father of 57 stone 11lb Daniel Lambert. On 11th February the Earl was taken to London and confined in the Tower. On 16th April 1760 the Earl's trial began in the House of Lords, Dr Kirkland being the chief witness for the prosecution.

The Earl's defence, apparently planned in advance by his family, was that his mental instability amounted to insanity and many people spoke about his strange behaviour – indeed, even his own brothers including the Rev. Walter Shirley spoke of his "unfraternal behaviour". In his summing up, the Solicitor General said that Ferrers had "convinced the peers of his sanity by the sense and sagacity with which he had conducted his defence". Each and every member of the House of Lords present then laid his hand on his breast and gave his verdict: "Guilty upon my honour". The Earl was sentenced to be hanged the following Monday, 21st April, and it was ordered that his body should be dissected and anatomised. (His execution was postponed and did not take place until 5th May).

No-one could recall a Peer of the Realm facing charges of this seriousness and the execution of an Earl was a momentous occasion. Selina tried to redeem her cousin by asking the King to deny him access to alcohol and playing cards while he was awaiting execution, but he gambled and drank to the last. Selina did however take his four daughters to see him on the day before his execution.

For his execution the Earl wore the white silk suit which he had worn on his wedding day because, as he put it, the day of his wedding and the day of his death were the two unhappiest days of his life. Contrary to popular belief, he was hanged with an ordinary rope, not a silk rope; but his family were anxious that he should not suffer the prolonged agony of death by strangulation and a special "drop" was invented, which later became standard at executions by hanging in Britain. At that time only the bodies of those who had been executed could legally be dissected by surgeons who were trying to find out more about the human anatomy and so by order of the Court the Earl's body was anatomised and examined by surgeons before it was interred, initially at St Pancras' Church in London, but in 1782 it was taken to Staunton Harold and buried in the family vault.

Laurence the 4th Earl Ferrers was the last Peer to be executed in England – but he might not have been. Only 5 years later another East Midlands peer, Lord Byron from Nottinghamshire, killed his neighbour William Chaworth in a drunken brawl over the best way to preserve game. He too was tried by the House of Lords but he was found guilty of manslaughter, not murder.

Good can come even out of a tragedy of this magnitude. It has been said that the execution of the 4th Earl Ferrers for the murder of his Steward proved that even an Earl was not above the law in England. This is given as one of the reasons why there was in England no equivalent of the French Revolution – the law in England applied to everyone and there was no need for a revolution to achieve justice.

It goes without saying that for many generations the Earl's family did not discuss this awful incident. Members of the family were told about it when they reached years of discretion but were forbidden from talking to others about it. Indeed, when a tradesman mentioned it at Staunton Harold on one occasion, he was shown the door and told never to return

And what of John Johnson? He is buried at Breedon and has a slate gravestone with the inscription:

Released from the evils of this frail world,
in pious expectation of the reward of his virtues
John Johnson
departed this life Jan XIX MDCCLX aged L
He was many years
the esteem'd and faithful servant
of
the Honble Laurence Shirley Esquire
with unshaken integrity
he continued in the office of Steward
to
his sone the late Right Honble Laurence Earl Ferrers
till near the fatal period of his life.
Uncorrupted by any views of self-interest,
no hopes no fears
Could divert him from the steady pursuit of that path
His duty to God and Man pointed out.
He was a worthy example of
The tender father, the affectionate husband,
The fair and valuable friend,
The sincere and humble Christian.
His many excellent Qualities
Rendered him highly Respected,
And his untimely Death
Much Lamented.

No word of accusation or recrimination! The cause of his death is not mentioned. Johnson was loyal to the last.

The Earl's estranged Countess, Mary, was married again, to Lord Frederick Campbell, 3rd son of the Duke of Argyll. She outlived Laurence for many years, but lost her life tragically in a fire in 1807.

SIMPLIFIED FAMILY TREE OF THE SHIRLEY FAMILY
Baronets and Earls Ferrers

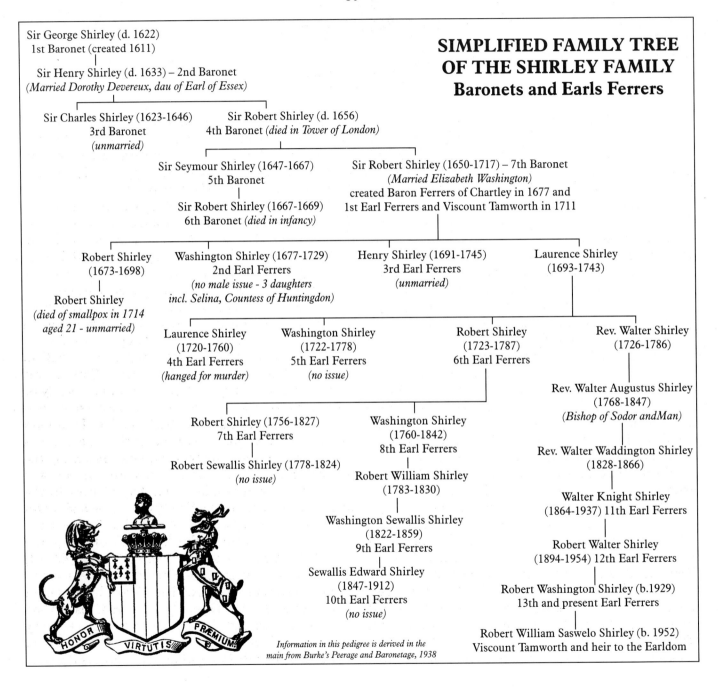

Sir George Shirley (d. 1622)
1st Baronet (created 1611)

Sir Henry Shirley (d. 1633) – 2nd Baronet
(Married Dorothy Devereux, dau of Earl of Essex)

Sir Charles Shirley (1623-1646)
3rd Baronet
(unmarried)

Sir Robert Shirley (d. 1656)
4th Baronet *(died in Tower of London)*

Sir Seymour Shirley (1647-1667)
5th Baronet

Sir Robert Shirley (1650-1717) – 7th Baronet
(Married Elizabeth Washington)
created Baron Ferrers of Chartley in 1677 and
1st Earl Ferrers and Viscount Tamworth in 1711

Sir Robert Shirley (1667-1669)
6th Baronet *(died in infancy)*

Robert Shirley
(1673-1698)

Robert Shirley
*(died of smallpox in 1714
aged 21 - unmarried)*

Washington Shirley (1677-1729)
2nd Earl Ferrers
*(no male issue - 3 daughters
incl. Selina, Countess of Huntingdon)*

Henry Shirley (1691-1745)
3rd Earl Ferrers
(unmarried)

Laurence Shirley
(1693-1743)

Laurence Shirley
(1720-1760)
4th Earl Ferrers
(hanged for murder)

Washington Shirley
(1722-1778)
5th Earl Ferrers
(no issue)

Robert Shirley
(1723-1787)
6th Earl Ferrers

Rev. Walter Shirley
(1726-1786)

Rev. Walter Augustus Shirley
(1768-1847)
(Bishop of Sodor and Man)

Robert Shirley (1756-1827)
7th Earl Ferrers

Washington Shirley
(1760-1842)
8th Earl Ferrers

Robert Sewallis Shirley (1778-1824)
(no issue)

Robert William Shirley
(1783-1830)

Rev. Walter Waddington Shirley
(1828-1866)

Washington Sewallis Shirley
(1822-1859)
9th Earl Ferrers

Walter Knight Shirley
(1864-1937) 11th Earl Ferrers

Sewallis Edward Shirley
(1847-1912)
10th Earl Ferrers
(no issue)

Robert Walter Shirley
(1894-1954) 12th Earl Ferrers

Robert Washington Shirley (b.1929)
13th and present Earl Ferrers

Robert William Saswelo Shirley (b. 1952)
Viscount Tamworth and heir to the Earldom

*Information in this pedigree is derived in the
main from Burke's Peerage and Baronetage, 1938*

HONOR VIRTUTIS PRÆMIUM

CHAPTER FOUR

THE HALL

*J*ohn Nichols was working on his definitive History and Antiquities of the County of Leicester at the very end of the 18th century. It was first published in 1804. The author of such a volume would at that time depend very heavily on the landed gentry to make his work a financial success, so Nichols was in a quandary about the events surrounding Laurence the 4th Earl Ferrers. Neither the Ferrers family nor any of their neighbours or peers would welcome details of the tragedy being perpetuated in the County's history. This probably explains why Nichols makes only the briefest and most tactful of references to the 4th Earl: "Leaving no issue, Earl Laurence was succeeded in 1760 by his next brother".

The 5th Earl, Washington, proved to be a most worthy holder of the title. He restored the family's fame and fortune and was largely responsible for the Staunton Harold Hall which exists today. "By his taste the splendid mansion at Staunton Harold was founded". The Hall which the 5th Earl bequeathed to posterity has been described as "one of the most beautifully proportioned and situated great houses in Britain" (AA Illustrated Guide to Britain 1976)

Little remains of the houses which had stood on the site in earlier centuries. There must have been substantial dwellings to house first the Stauntons and later the Shirleys, but almost all trace of them has now disappeared, though a few parts of the medieval house are incorporated into the present Hall. The first house of significance at Staunton is said to have been built around 1324. Francis Shirley, who purchased Breedon Church from Henry VIII, also built an Elizabethan mansion at Staunton around 1566, which was described as having two turrets and Gothic entrance gates, towers and a gatehouse. It was said that the previous mansion was sparsely furnished and cold, but the new mansion was lavishly equipped and possessed "a gloomy grandeur". (H.J.Wain)

Sir Henry, the second Baronet, was a devout Roman Catholic and had a private chapel in the Hall. This chapel still exists and is said to be part of the old Hall – possible even of the original Hall. It has 12 portraits of Saints, probably copies of works by Flemish artists who painted the originals between the 15th and 18th centuries: the copies may have been painted by a local artist around 1790. There is also a frieze of cherubs' heads, unique except that the same design was used on Sir Henry's "high pew" of 1627 in Breedon Church. In 1614 Sir George Shirley was granted permission to hold Courts Leet (i.e. yearly or half-yearly courts of record) in Leicestershire and Derbyshire, and at one time this little chapel was used as the Justice Room, where the Earl would act in a magisterial capacity to settle matters concerning the estate and his tenants. But more recently the room was made into a non-denominational chapel for use by the staff and residents in the Sue Ryder Home and it was furnished and arranged as it was in the 17th century.

A notable feature in this little Chapel within the Sue Ryder Home was an alabaster head of Christ, inspired by the Turin Shroud, which was presented to Group Captain Cheshire and Lady Ryder by the Isle of Wight artist, Mrs Ross Spencer. Leonard Cheshire had become a Roman Catholic and was greatly impressed by the Shroud, a picture of which featured in a bus in which he toured Britain raising funds for his Homes.

Above: The Justice Room/Chapel
Right: Part of the central courtyard.

The Elizabethan Hall served the family well for a century but was extensively rebuilt by Robert, the 1st Earl. Robert was described by a contemporary as "a very honest man; a lover of his country; a great improver of gardening and parking; a keen sportsman; never yet in business, but is very capable". He completed the building of the Chapel which had been started by his father Robert, the 4th Baronet. In 1711 the beautiful iron screen in the Chapel and the Golden Gates were made by Robert Bakewell of Derby for the Earl.

The building for which the 1st Earl was responsible can be seen clearly in Kip's engraving of the Hall, which was produced in 1702. The "Library" front, which became the Sue Ryder Coffee and Gift Shop, was the main entrance to the Hall until the 1760s. Complete architectural symmetry proved impossible to obtain because of the nature of the earlier buildings, but the Earl obtained symmetry in the grounds by

Outside the Justice Room/Chapel is a colonnade which features Tuscan columns. This would have been planted as a courtyard garden. The stone wall and mullioned windows were exposed during the restoration and are clearly part of the old Manor House.

laying out fine formal terraced gardens well watered with fountains and with a canal which was said to be the largest in Leicestershire. These gardens are very clear in 18th century paintings of Staunton Harold. The gardens by the Lion Front (more recently known as the Lion Court) have been well reconstructed with help from Leicestershire County Council so that they resemble the original design by the 1st Earl, who was advised by George London, Head Gardener to King William III and designer of the gardens at Melbourne Hall.

The formal 18th century gardens can be seen in Kip's engraving but were swept away by the 5th Earl early in the reign of George III. *Country Life* said in 1913: "the walled gardens, bowling greens, hedges and terraces, canals and fountains, statuary and vases all disappeared as completely as the baseless fabric of dreams, leaving only the magnificent gate-piers, surmounted by the Talbot and Stag, the Shirley supporters, which once led to the bowling green". It was the 1st Earl who commissioned these superb baroque gate-piers which greet visitors as they

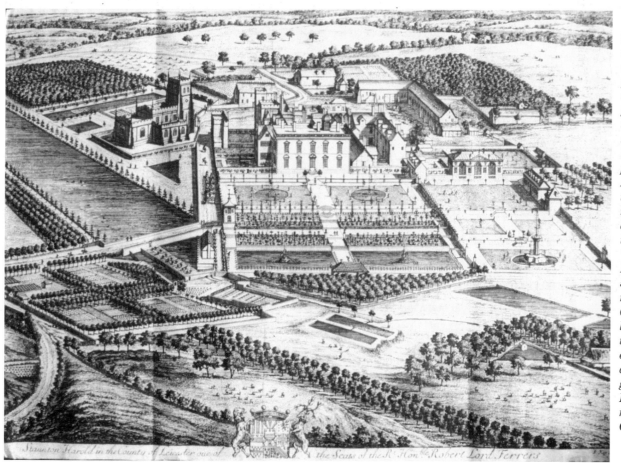

Kip's engraving, dating from 1702, of the Hall, gardens and surrounding parkland. At that time the main entrance was in the 'Library Front'. The 5th Earl's renovations 60 years later moved the entrance to a new and grander East Front near the Chapel.

approach Staunton along the direct drive from the Melbourne to Ashby road. These gate-piers, which have been moved from their original location near the bowling green, are now the responsibility of the National Trust. They used to carry the magnificent Golden Gates, which now hang outside the home of the present Earl in Norfolk

Another superb gateway from the garden and bearing the date 1681 has been moved to its present position immediately to the right of the chapel gates, where it is also in the care of the National Trust. "This gateway, with its heavy rustication, cornucopias and huge flower-filled urn at the top, is particularly interesting as a piece of pattern-book architecture, based on a plate in the English edition of "Vignola", published by Joseph Moxon on 1655". (National Trust).

The 1st Earl, while he was still the 7th Baronet between 1670 and 1675, also furnished the house in a style befitting his restored status. He liked pictures and paid £10-15-0d (£10.75p) for a painting of the Countess of Shrewsbury, 32/- (£1.60p) for a "great landscape" and 14/- (70p) for a "small landscape", and even 14/- (70p) for a "piece of birds". He and his wife had to dress

The Golden Gates at Staunton Harold hanging on the baroque gate-piers.

and live in the right manner too and their household expenses included £3 for a coral necklace for his wife, £1-2-0d (£1.10p) for a dozen pairs of white gloves and "for my lady's twilight and nightgowns" £13-19-0d (£13.95p). For himself a runlet (21 gallons) of sack cost 8 guineas (£8.40p), 1lb of Spanish tobacco cost 12/- (60p) and a perriwig set him back £20!

But it was the 5th Earl, Washington, who created Staunton as we know it today. He had not expected to inherit the title. He had entered the navy as a midshipman and had served with great distinction, rising through the ranks to become a Vice-Admiral: he was made a Fellow of the Royal Society on 14th December 1761 for work on the transit of the planet Venus. Washington inherited the title and estate from his brother Laurence in 1760. He employed a well-known local architect, William Henderson, as his Clerk of Works and Paymaster for 9 years from 1762. He extended the main east front of the Hall and he also created the Lion Front.

Nichols, writing in 1804, says: "The south-east, or grand front, is in the style of Palladio; the pediment supported by Ionic pillars, and those again upheld by columns of the Doric order. The centre of this front is stone, the red brick ornamented with stone. On the pediment stand three lively figures from the antique. [leaden figures of Minerva, Apollo and Ceres] On the other parts of the mansion are also some spirited casts, one of which is an exceedingly large lion, on the south-west front. This front is very extensive, and built

The east or Grand Front of Staunton Harold Hall, looking out over the lake and to the chapel.

in the form of a Roman H. On the north east is the library front, originally designed by Inigo Jones and nearly preserved in the present structure".

Those familiar with Staunton Harold today will readily recognise it from this description, though it should be noted that there is no evidence to support the claim that Inigo Jones was involved at Staunton.

A village which had grown up around the old house was demolished to make way for the great mansion and all its outbuildings. It is not certain where this village was or exactly when it was moved. It may have been moved at this time but it has been suggested by John Blunt that the village may have been located near the conduit house in the park and that it may have been cleared for sheep farming as early as the 14th century.

It was the 5th Earl who changed the character of the gardens, sweeping away the formal gardens laid out by the 1st Earl, enlarging the lakes and making them softer in appearance.

All of this work was very expensive: for example, the Earl paid £54-14-0d (£54.70p) for 203,000 bricks. Although he was receiving £1-0-7d (£1.03p) per ton for the coal which was mined on the estate, the Earl had to sell some of the family's property to finance the alterations at Staunton Harold. Brailsford in Derbyshire was sold for £88,000, but this was not enough and so he sold his 1,963 acre estate at Astwell and Falcutt in Northamptonshire, to finance the alterations at Staunton Harold, his principal seat. It is not known exactly how much the Earl obtained for Astwell and Falcutt when it was bought by Richard Grenville, 2nd Earl Temple to extend his Stowe property, but it was in the region of 28 times the annual rent i.e. in excess of £36,000, but still well below Earl Ferrer's original asking price of £45,796.

The interior of the Hall has not normally been open to the public since the Hall became a Sue Ryder Home though the former LIBRARY became the Coffee Shop and the PARLOUR became the Gift Shop, and both gave visitors some idea of its splendour. The LIBRARY still has all its shelving, which was ideal for displaying items illustrating some of Sue Ryder's work throughout the world. It was formerly furnished with 18th century elegance, but very little of the family furniture now remains.

The PARLOUR or Drawing Room was used for family entertainment especially when the family had no visitors. They used the top fireplace for warmth on these occasions and screened off the remaining area. This was also the room where the family took high tea and where Lady Ferrers was "at home".

The ENTRANCE HALL, with its doorway facing the Chapel, has been the main entrance to the Hall since the 1760's: prior to that the main entrance led into what became the Library. There is a Tudor cupboard and a 19th century sideboard in the entrance hall.

Opening off the entrance hall is the magnificent EARL'S DINING ROOM, with a painting of the 10th Earl over the fireplace. The 10th Earl spent his own fortune and that of his wife Ina, an Irish Countess, on the refurbishment of Staunton Harold, including the panelling in this room. In order to achieve the symmetry which was then fashionable, he put two false doors in this room. The family motto over the fireplace reads: "HONOR VIRTUTIS PRAEMIUM" (Honour is the reward of Virtue).

Adjacent to the Earl's Dining Room is the 10th Earl's DEN. An engraving on one of the wooden window shutters says that "this room was inaugurated on 8th May 1875 by the cigars of W. Woodroffe, F.H.Walsh, Ferrers". This room became the office of the Health Care Services of Sue Ryder Care. A spiral staircase gives easy access from the den to the Earl's bedroom apartments above.

Above left: The Earl's Dining Room
Above right: The 10th Earl's portrait over the fireplace.

In the 10th Earl's time there were 40 indoor and 40 outdoor staff. Many of them were photographed between 1900 and 1912, each one being shown with an appropriate "tool of their trade" – the joiner is holding a saw, the woodsman is shown with an axe, the scullery maid is carrying a basket, the waggoner is holding a whip and the messenger boy has his bicycle.

A passage behind the dining room leads to the Lion Court and there is still a rack where the family kept tools with which they enjoyed doing some work in a part of the garden known as the Wilderness: despite the number of outdoor staff, the staff were not allowed to touch the Wilderness. One of the gardeners at the beginning of the 20th century was Job Watson, who is said to have found it difficult to keep awake during long sermons in the Chapel and was therefore one of several people who had to be prodded by the verger with a pole which was kept for this purpose.

Another corridor, now giving access to offices, is still known as the LAMP CORRIDOR, as it was here that Little Tom Shaw and others employed as "Trimmers of the Oil Lamps" would undertake their vital task. (This Tom Shaw was always known as "Little" because there was another Tom Shaw known as "Long" on the staff at the same time!)

A staircase-hall was built c. 1764 and from it a superb STAIRCASE (see page 24) leads to the first floor. The ironwork with its elaborate acanthus leafed lyre pattern is probably the work of Benjamin Yates, who made several staircases of a similar design for other houses in the Midlands. The ceiling painting is of the Venetian school. The portrait of the Earl of Sussex at the time of King George IV's coronation is still owned by the Ferrers family.

Left: Head staff housemaid from the early 20th century, in her uniform.

Below: Nurse Gibbons preparing lamps for use in the Cheshire Home. Electricity was not installed in Staunton Harold until 1956/7.

Upstairs the SALOON is one of the finest rooms in the Hall. It is in a mixture of styles, with a neo-classical fireplace and Palladian doorcases, which unfortunately have been painted over. As in the Earl's Dining Room, there are two fake doors for the sake of symmetry. The plasterwork dates from the 17th century and the ceiling painting is attributed to Cipriani. This room was known by the family as the Saloon but became known as the State Room when it was taken into use for Day Care Services by Sue Ryder Care.

All the most important rooms in Staunton have significant fireplaces. In the Saloon the fireplace is made of locally mined alabaster inlaid with Blue John from Derbyshire and surrounded with fine hand-painted tiles. There is another fine marble fireplace in the Parlour which became the Sue Ryder shop. The fireplace in the entrance hall is decorated with bulls' skulls and the fireplace in the Earl's Dining Room is decorated with horse-shoes, the significance of which will be explained later.

The suites and bedrooms were all used by residents in the Sue Ryder Home. Some still bear the names of the members of the family who last lived in the Hall – Lady Hermione, Lady Elizabeth, Lady Penelope and Lady Phillida. But one is known as the Ghost Suite as it is said to be where John Johnson was murdered. The children's bedrooms were with the rest of the family on the first floor, with domestic staff rooms on the top floor.

A staircase leads to the servants' hall which was panelled, but the panelling was torn out, probably for fuel by Second World War Italian prisoners of war who were lodged in the Hall. This is believed to be another of the rooms of the earlier manor house.

There are many other rooms including a brewhouse and dairy, now used for storage and as a workshop. The kitchen was used as an exhibition area but now has been converted into an excellent meeting/lecture room.

The Saloon furnished for use as a Sue Ryder Day Care Centre.

The extensive range of cellars includes separate Ale and Beer cellars, the difference being that hops are used in the brewing of beer but not in ale. As well as being Trimmer of the Oil Lamps, Little Tom Shaw was also Brewer of the estate beer.

There were also far more extensive buildings outside the Hall than there are now, including an Orangery in which the 10th Earl posed for some "tropical" photographs. The massive stable building has become the Ferrers Centre for Arts and Crafts, about which more will be said later.

In the programme for the tercentenary celebrations of the Chapel in 1953, it was written: "Throughout its long history, Staunton Harold has frequently been reshaped to meet contemporary needs. It would still serve a modern purpose. Just as the Commonwealth church and the Georgian house stand side by side in harmony, so good contemporary work could blend into this perfect setting to fulfil the requirements of a modern use".

The first modern user was the Cheshire Foundation, founded by Group Captain Leonard Cheshire V.C., D.S.O.,D.F.C. Leonard Cheshire had been an outstanding bomber pilot during the second World War. He was an official British observer when the atomic bomb was dropped on Nagasaki in 1945 and this experience, together with his conversion to Roman Catholicism, made him devote the rest of his life to tending the sick by founding Cheshire Homes in Britain and in many other countries. When the Cheshire Home residents were moved away from Staunton Harold in the 1980s, the Hall was taken over for use by Sue Ryder Care, a charitable foundation established by Lady Sue Ryder of Warsaw, Leonard Cheshire's wife. Sue Ryder had also distinguished herself during the Second World War, serving with the Special Operations Executive, through which she saw the terrible suffering of many people in Poland and elsewhere. After the war she established a Foundation to be a "living memorial to the victims and opponents of tyranny and to those who suffer and die as a result of persecution". Since then the Sue Ryder Foundation has grown in size and in the scope of the help it offers to people in need. In turn, both of these charities have used the Hall and its surroundings for the benefit of people in need. No doubt those who designed and built the Hall, and all who have lived and worked in the buildings throughout the ages, would today be delighted that many still enjoy and benefit from the peace and beauty at Staunton Harold.

CHAPTER FIVE

THE ESTATE

*T*he Staunton Harold Estate was very extensive: in 1804 Nichols said that it consisted of 1,700 acres in a beautiful valley "from the very meer of Derbyshire, from which county it is separated by a brook which runs out of a fine sheet of water in front of the house". At that time the average annual rent for cornland, woodland and meadows was 22/- (£.1.10p). There were 52 houses of various sorts on the estate, including the colliers' houses at Lount. Sand and lime, coal and some lead had already been found and the price of coal had risen from 6/- (30p) to £1 per load.

The earliest mention of a park at Staunton occurs in a charter dated 22nd April 1324, whereby Sir William de Staunton granted a house and land at Staunton to Walter Clowne of Melbourne for an annual rent of 10/- (50p) plus 4 hens at Christmas and the work of hedging in Staunton Park, wherein Sir William covenanted to build a principal house and grange by Michaelmas.

It may have been on the site of that grange that Francis Shirley built a keeper's lodge in 1566, for Francis spent much of his time hunting in the Great Park. This lodge was a moated half-timbered house which stood off the Ashby-Breedon road and was demolished in the 19th century but has been rebuilt. The moat is still intact.

In 1584 Sir George Shirley appointed Joseph Crisp as his park keeper with a licence to kill deer. It appears that Joseph Crisp lived in the house called the "lodge" within the park.

Sir Henry Shirley, the second Baronet, was a keen falconer who spent much of his time in the Great Park

Ashby Lodge on the Staunton Harold estate, providing access to the Hall from near Lount.

Mrs Smith, Keeper of the Gate at Melbourne Lodge, early in the 20th century.

which, however, he "disparked" in 1623, dividing the land into farms – a first step towards "enclosure" in many parts of England at that time.

In addition to the Great Park, there was a smaller deer park attached to the mansion, which was reduced in size by the fifth Earl Ferrers when he rebuilt the Hall and remodelled the gardens in the late 18th century. There were plenty of fish in the lake and ponds, and Nichols records that at the time of the Countess of Huntingdon's wedding in 1728 a carp was dressed which weighed 24 lbs.

H.J.Wain recorded much of the above information about the estate, but also added his own personal memories:

"At the beginning of the present century my grandfather lived at Calke Mill. As a boy I had the run of the Staunton estate, which was then a naturalist's paradise. Although game was reared on a large scale and rats and other "vermin" were destroyed, many birds found sanctuary there.

"The park comprises 150 acres with a lake of 25 acres. At the beginning of the 20th century it contained 100 fallow deer, the average weight of a buck being 95lbs and of a doe 55lbs. There were also 10 red deer in the park. The herd of deer was killed off in 1933.

"The park contained many oak trees with hollow limbs, which provided nesting places for owls, kestrels, jackdaws, stockdoves, nuthatches, tits, and other hole-nesting birds. There was a large rookery in tall beech trees on the boundary of the park, while swans, great crested grebes, coots, moorhens and wild ducks nested on the banks of the lake, which was frequented by a variety of wildfowl during the winter months. Kingfishers and grey wagtails nested in the banks of the stream.

"In the adjacent Spring Wood a large variety of songbirds found nesting places, as well as woodpigeons and woodcock. In 1915 the nest of a teal, our smallest

British duck, was found there and the young were successfully reared.

"In 1904 a small party of terns or "sea-swallows" frequented the lake for several days, and a white swallow was seen in 1912. In the latter year a Chinese goose built her nest on an island in the stream flowing past the gamekeeper's cottage. A fox swam across, killed the goose, smashed the eggs on a boulder and devoured the unhatched goslings".

Mr Wain's grandfather was a friend of Samuel Greatbach, a large man with a bushy beard who was paid 16/- (80p) a week as Head Gamekeeper at Staunton Harold. Samuel also had a suit of clothes provided and a special uniform of dark green cloth ornamented with silver buttons bearing the Ferrers' horseshoe. Game was preserved in the traditional manner for large shooting parties and the Police helped the keepers to protect the game from poachers.

The 10th Earl maintained a pack of hounds and the most spectacular building he erected at Staunton is now called Hunt Lodge. It was built to house the hounds of the Quorn Hunt which was going through a difficult time in the 1870s. John Blunt writes: "When we bought them in 1955 the kennels still had the iron-railed exercise yards in front of them: some of the railings are now round my own small dog kennel in Melbourne. The building then became a cow-shed with a cattery above before being substantially restored and turned into four houses".

It was not only the game and the Park which were well tended. The family looked after the whole estate well. Between 1670 and 1675 Sir Robert the fifth Baronet paid £10-16-0d (£10.80p) for "English trees" to Young the gardener: 80 plum trees cost £2-13-4d (£2.66p), 80 cherry trees cost the same, 12 peach and nectarine trees cost £1-4-0d (£1.20p), and 3 mulberry trees cost 10/- (50p). He also paid £5 for 10 orange trees

Samuel Greatbach, wearing the uniform of Head Gamekeeper and carrying a double-barrelled shotgun as a symbol of his office.

and £3 for 6 lemon trees, which were probably put in the hot houses.

Wain said that in his youth the gardens, farms and stockyards were patterns of efficiency. The large household was a training centre for domestic servants and the Home Farm was a model of its kind.

The staff were always well looked after. The 12th Earl gave two leather armchairs to those who got married and his Countess gave them a china breakfast and tea service.

But the estate was not only agricultural. Coal and iron had been worked on the Staunton estate since the 14th century, and at the end of the 18th century coal and iron, lead and copper and lime of excellent quality could be mined. In 1794 an Act of Parliament was obtained for the construction of a canal to the South Derbyshire coalfields, with extensions to Ticknall and Breedon, but this proved impracticable and a tramway was constructed instead. The trucks were drawn by horses over iron rails fastened to stone blocks. In 1828,

The former Staunton Estate is still an area of beautiful woods and farmland.

at the request of Earl Ferrers, a branch of the Ticknall tramway was constructed from South Wood to his limeworks in Dimminsdale at the edge of Staunton park. The selected route was on Sir George Crewe's estate on the Derbyshire side of the stream which forms the county boundary, and the route of that tramway is now being turned into a footpath by the National Trust.

In 1846 the Midland Railway Company obtained an Act of Parliament to construct a railway from Burton-on-Trent to Nuneaton with branches to the Swadlincote collieries and potteries on condition that the Company purchased the existing canal and its tramways and maintained them in working order. These were acquired for £110,000 and the Staunton line continued in use until 1891.

The Hall had its own water supply and was not connected to the main water system until the 1950s. There is therefore a touch of irony about the fact that, in 1955, approval was given to a scheme to construct a dam to create a reservoir in the valley between Staunton Harold and Melbourne: by 1963/4 water was being supplied from this reservoir to meet the increasing demand in Leicestershire. Calke Mill and farmhouse and Furnace Farm were submerged by the reservoir and new roads had to be constructed.

When the Hall was sold in 1954, the estate was fragmented and it is now owned by various parties. Church Pool, opposite the Hall, and the Wilderness Wood were sold with the Hall and became the property of the Leonard Cheshire Foundation.

The walled gardens were bought by Stanley and Dorothy Watson and were converted into a garden centre almost by accident. Stan was making a modest living in the gardens, growing plants and selling them at nearby wholesale markets. Occasionally he would make a sale direct from the nursery and John Blunt recalls that "he put the cash in the small space under the lid of an old marble mantle clock which lived in the first greenhouse. If there was £5 in there at the day's end he had done very well and I remember him telling me that he had no wish to expand".

But in the early 1970s things began to look up in the wider world. Many more people had cars and the fashion grew for families to take trips out to buy their garden plants direct from the nurseries. With his easy-going charm and the chance of picking up a bargain, the nursery became a Mecca and Stan was too good a businessman to turn trade away. The extra traffic made other demands and Stan Watson paid for the building of car parks and the tarmacking of some roads, as the Cheshire Home had paid for others to be tarmacked earlier.

The three tenanted farms at the centre of the estate, totalling 550 acres, had failed to sell at auction in 1954. They were then advertised on the opening page of *Country Life* for £45,000. John Blunt recalls that his father embarked on drawn-out negotiations with the agents. Eventually the new (13th) Earl Ferrers himself went to see Mr Blunt and the sale was made. The purchase included all the parkland around the Hall, most of the estate roads and the derelict stables behind the Hall which have been converted into the Ferrers Centre for Arts and Crafts: more will be said later about how this development has taken place over the last half century.

CHAPTER SIX

THE FERRERS FAMILY IN MORE RECENT TIMES

*A*fter the 5th Earl, for several generations the family lived in style and contributed to the well-being of their own community and nation without becoming either famous or notorious. Perhaps this was wise after all the traumas they had experienced in the 17th and 18th centuries! The 5th Earl, Washington, died childless in 1778 and was succeeded by his brother Robert who died in 1787. Robert's son, another Robert, inherited the title and died in 1827, when he was succeed by his brother Washington, who died in 1842. Washington's grandson was the 9th Earl until 1859, when he was succeeded by his 12 year old son Sewallis as the 10th Earl. Sewallis was the head of the family for 53 years, and in that long period he had a great effect on Staunton Harold and on the family's fortunes. He was the last member of the family to live in great style, his footmen having powdered heads and wearing silk stockings, with silver horseshoes on their sleeves. The housekeepers (Mrs Mellish, followed by Miss Bailey from 1900 to 1910) wore traditional black silk dresses with gold chains round their necks and tucked into their belts. Even tea was served with perfect ritual by a butler and three powdered footmen.

The 9th Earl had married Lady Augusta Annabella Chichester, daughter of Edward 4th Marquess of Donegall. Their son Sewallis graduated from Trinity College Cambridge in 1867. He did not marry until 1885, when he was 38 years old: his bride was another Irish Lady, Ina Maud White, daughter of the 3rd Earl of Bantry.

The 10th Earl Ferrers came into his inheritance as a young man in 1859 and lived at Staunton Harold in considerable style until his death in 1912. He played a full part in local affairs over a very wide area, being a Magistrate in Derbyshire and a Magistrate and Deputy Lieutenant for Leicestershire and Staffordshire. He was a member of Leicestershire County Council. He is said to have regretted seeing politics become increasingly influenced by party spirit rather than by patriotic feeling. He was a Fellow of the Zoological and Botanical Societies and a member of the Royal Agricultural Society. He enjoyed sport, especially cricket and golf: he had his own golf-course and employed a professional. He was an enthusiastic long-range rifle shot and for several years took part in contests at Wimbledon for the Lords v. Commons.

Miss Bailey, Housekeeper at Staunton Harold in the early years of the 20th century.

The Earl comes across as a rather morose man, bound up in his estate despite his public commitments. Ina enjoyed poor health and lived a rather lonely life. They had no children. There is an excellent cameo of life at Staunton in those years in the autobiography of Katherine Everett entitled *Bricks and Flowers*. Katherine (nee Herbert) was an Irish woman whose cousin Ina had married the 10th Earl. In her autobiography "Bricks and Flowers" (an apt title, for she became a landscape gardener) she gives a vivid impression of Staunton Harold when she visited her cousin in about 1890 and stayed for several months at a young and impressionable age as a companion to the Countess Ferrers. Her own family were quite poor and she was completely overawed by the grandeur of the Hall and the style in which they lived. She describes how each afternoon the head butler in full livery would enter the Saloon and announce tea and then stand at the door while a succession of servants brought in the food.

Katherine wrote about being shown around the estate, sometimes by the estate nurse, at other times by the agent. With the nurse she learned how well everyone was cared for, from the babies to the very elderly. She concludes by describing the life of the people under the Earl's care as the most contented she had encountered in a long career and many travels.

Katherine Everett, aged 12, from her Memoirs, 'Bricks and Flowers'.

Katherine showed an interest in the whole estate and was impressed by the care with which the staff were trained. The housekeeper said of her girls; *"If we don't promote them here when they are trained we find them good places, but most of them get married after they have been with us a few years, and they make good wives, for they know how their homes and children should be kept".*

With the agent Katherine visited the stables full of horses, including heavy horses for working the land. At the Home Farm she saw the herd of shorthorn cattle, all of the very best bloodlines. At the head gamekeeper's cottage she saw the lines of coops for hatching and rearing pheasants and he told her that the Earl could show as good a day's sport as any estate in England. The head gardener's mantelpiece was laden with trophies. He had 8 men and 6 boys working under him and was enormously proud that boys he had trained and placed had done well: *"One boy of mine is well up at Kew, while another is head at the Duke of D...'s"*. Everywhere Katherine went the tasks were done to the highest standards and with pride in their performance.

Many stories are told about the 10th Earl, and some of them may be apocryphal. But Katherine Everett recorded some incidents which show that life at Staunton Harold in late Victorian times was out of the ordinary. She gives a particularly endearing account of the ritual which took place on Sundays.

"I was told to be ready in the hall at five minutes to eleven, where I found two processions drawn up on either side of the stuffed bull, one headed by the house-keeper, with all the maids behind her, dressed in black with little black bonnets, and on the other side the butler and menservants, no longer in their eighteenth-century dress, but all in dark suits.

"I stayed at the back of the hall while a bell was ringing from the church across the gravel and everyone stood quite still. Then Ferrers came, looking slighter than ever, and wearing a tail coat and carrying a top hat. Deviating for the bull, he walked between the ranks of servants to the hall door, which at that moment was opened by an elderly man carrying a black velvet

cushion on which was a large key, who came in and stood behind Ferrers. The housekeeper darted towards me whispering, "Walk beside his lordship and stay with him", and then she led the maids to the church, followed by the men, and lastly by Ferrers, who put on his top hat as he crossed the gravel.

"The church seemed fairly full, the women sitting on one side and the men on the other. Inside we paused for a moment while the man with the cushion locked the door and led us to the front pew, placing the key on a shelf in front of us, and as soon as this was done the bell stopped and an old clergyman came in and read the service in a slow, droning voice. It seemed dull until Ferrers whispered to me, "Stand up", while everyone else was kneeling, and I heard the slow voice add to the prayers for the Royal Family, 'And for Sewallis, Earl Ferrers, Ina Maude, Countess Ferrers, the Lady Augusta Palmer, the Earl's sister, and Katherine Herbert, the Countess's cousin'. I felt horribly self-conscious, and when the prayers were over subsided onto my footstool uncertain if I was going to laugh or cry.

"Everyone left the church before we did and then the door was locked and the key returned to its caretaker.

"Later I asked Ina what happened to the clergyman. 'He's locked in the church, but we feed him – if you look out of the window you will see his luncheon going in. Also', she added with a smile, 'what the French call a chaise percee [commode], and at three he takes a children's service, and the evening service at four, after which he is let out. Ferrers doesn't like him, for he neglects the people and doesn't trouble if anyone is ill, but although it's our private chapel and not under the Bishop's jurisdiction, we can't get rid of him, as he won't resign.'

"I did look out of the window, and saw a procession going to the church, headed by the man with the key, followed by objects held on poles. It looked like an old illustration of the Ark of the Covenant"

Katherine found some of the pomp and formality at Staunton Harold *"a little absurd"*. But she was also clearly impressed by the *"fine side to a tradition that was unbroken for generations – a tradition of mutual obligations and service recognised by all, from the owner to the humblest dependant. There existed a bond of pride and love of the place among them all, pride perhaps more actively felt by the employees in their various departments than by the owner, and everyone was assured of comfort and security. "Such places have almost ceased to exist in England"*, she concluded, *"yet I can think of no group of human beings in any present-day setting to compare with this estate where, as in many others, the mutual feeling was so kindly and where there existed an almost communal enjoyment of the expenditure of wealth".*

But however justified it may have been in human terms, all that expenditure was really too much for the estate to bear. When Katherine commented on the excellent conditions in which the livestock was kept, the estate manager told her: *"A working farmer could not do this, for he has to take the short view and can't afford risks. But it pays a fine dividend in other ways than making money, for every tenant on this estate and many an outsider have benefited by what we have done. It is people who have the will and the means who have raised the level of British farming".*

When Katherine asked whether farming in this way paid she was told: *"Not in straightforward terms, but we help our farm tenants by giving them access to good bloodlines and buying things like seed in bulk so that they can afford better quality. And everything is accounted for, including all the things which go to be used in the big house".* That was as much as Katherine could learn on the subject but we can surmise that those accounts were showing a steady loss and that eventually the whole edifice would collapse.

But surely something would turn up? After all, the family had been through some sticky patches during the last 400 years and always pulled through somehow. It seemed reasonable to expect that after a run of bad farming years something would happen to restore the family finances.

This time there was to be no salvation. Instead things got worse. For every landed family in England, the next half century produced very little to cheer about. The introduction of Death Duties (now called the Inheritance Tax) hit them hard. The First World War took men away from the estate, never to return on anything like the scale of the 10th Earl's time. It was then, according to John Blunt's father, that the deer escaped from the park below the Hall and were not recaptured, leaving one bank to an invasion of bracken and scrub which is only now being reversed.

The 10th Earl had no children and when he died in 1912 the title and estate were inherited by Walter Knight, a practising architect and a descendant of the Rev. Walter Shirley the 18th century cleric and hymnwriter. The 10th Earl had overspent and the family was not well off. The 11th Earl and his Countess Jane themselves did far more than their predecessor had done: she took responsibility for running the Hall, while the Earl was active on the estate. H.J.Wain tells the tale of an occasion when a couple of workmen were having difficulty in repairing a gate and the Earl stopped to lend them a hand. The Earl moved aside to let a tradesman pass: "Thanks my man" said the tradesman, who was new to the district, and tossed the Earl a shilling (5p).

But there were still family traits which appealed to those who knew them. In the diaries of James Lees-Milne (from the family who lived at nearby Calke Abbey) the following tale appears: *"Eardly told me yesterday that when he was a boy at Winchester he stayed with a school friend Andrew Shirley, at his home Staunton Harold. The house even in those days, about 1917, was half closed, rooms under dust-sheets. The father Lord Ferrers had a black labrador of which he was extremely fond. Each morning on the portico he gave a peculiar order to the dog, which bounded away over the fields and through a wood. It made for the main London-to-Leicester (sic) railway line which ran through the Staunton Harold estate a mile off. The guard on the train from London would at a certain spot throw a copy of The Times out of the window. The dog caught it and brought it back in its mouth to his master. This was a regular matutinal procedure"*.

Writing under the heading "Down Memory Lane" in 1967, the Dowager Countess Ferrers recorded her impressions of life at Staunton Harold as it was in the days before, during and after the Second World War. These memoirs were printed in a booklet compiled and published by Mrs Drucella Starkey entitled "The Cheshire Home at Staunton Harold". Great changes have taken place since then in society at large as well as at Staunton Harold and these memoirs reveal so much about the age to which they refer that it is right that they should again be made available to the public.

The Dowager Countess wrote as follows: *"My husband and I spent many long visits there with the children before it was his turn to succeed. (in 1937)*

"My earliest recollections of Staunton Harold are of a very beautiful home – full of love and full of history – and there was a curious feeling that the family belonged to Staunton Harold and not that Staunton Harold belonged to them. There was a strong sense of ritual and the order of precedence was always observed – strict punctuality throughout the day was fundamental. This was aided by a very loud bell on the roof, which was rung twice before every meal – the first, 10 minutes before the appointed time, the second five minutes later. It was the custom for all to assemble before going in to a meal.

"Six mornings in the week Family Prayers were conducted by Lord Ferrers (the 11th Earl) at 8.50 in the Dining-room. After 10 or 15 minutes of very beautiful reading and praying, the staff filed out to their various work, while we all sat down to a huge breakfast. The days were fully occupied with countless activities – riding, shooting, fishing, gardening and farming, visiting and being visited, reading and writing and a variety of functions to attend. I remember so well one day at the end of lunch Lady Ferrers saying, "Tonight, ladies, we will all wear our lace" – and a truly lovely sight it was, and very interesting to look at. We always went in to dinner arm in arm, Lord Ferrers announced the names of each couple in the drawing room and then, the gong sounded loud and long, the doors were thrown open – dinner was announced and the procession moved off. Grace was said by Lord Ferrers, in Latin, then followed by a lovely dinner, all lit by candles and lamps which seemed to make an ideal end to the day's happiness. Large fires burned in so many rooms – they were the only means of heating this big house.

"In those days there was ample time to indulge in all kinds of crafts – lace-making, embroidery, tapestry, sewing, knitting, tatting, tenting, patchwork – we often did these by candle-light and lamp-light after dinner; or we would play games – puff billiards, bagatelle, backgammon, draughts, chess, card games and all sorts of guessing games, dumb crambo and charades were great fun – and we played the piano and sang. We were always doing things. (Today so much is done for us – on the TV and wireless, when we just sit and watch and make no effort, and sometimes fall asleep)

"Sundays were always faithfully observed with the utmost devotion – services were regularly held in the lovely "Private Chapel" as it was then – attended by the people living on the estate, the staff and the family. All had their special pew to go to, the ladies always on the left of the centre aisle and the men on the right. Lady

The 12th Earl and his family by the lake at Staunton Harold (Picture courtesy of the Leicester Mercury)

Ferrers and her daughter sat in the front pew, behind them came the Chaplain's wife and daughter, followed by the school mistress, then the housekeeper and domestic staff in order of seniority. On the other side, Lord Ferrers and his son sat in the front pew, and behind them came the Chaplain's son, followed by the Steward, the head gardener, the butler, and so on. A glorious peal of bells rang out over the Park for a quarter of an hour.

"It was the custom for the tenants and staff to be in the Church five minutes before the appointed time of the service. When the single bell (known as the five minutes' bell) stopped, the family walked from the front door to the Church – led by Lady Ferrers. Lord Ferrers came last on these occasions because he always locked the West door after he had entered, so that no one could ever come in late. The keys were then placed on a velvet cushion, which the Clerk carried, followed by Lord Ferrers, to the front pew. When the service was over, the *keys were collected and the West door was unlocked by the Clerk, so that the congregation went out first, the family last. Three times on Sundays did this happen. There was always a Celebration at 8 a.m., Mattins at 11 and Evensong at 6.p.m. Lord Ferrers always read the lessons. He was a very beautiful reader. He told me he read the lessons over in Greek before reading them in Church.*

"So the ritual and precedence never really broke down – it seemed to be part of Staunton. In 1937 Lord Ferrers died. His body was laid to rest in the little Church Garden.

"My husband and I went to live at Staunton – our children grew up to love this house so deeply. They loved the people on the estate, they loved every bit of the house, garden and wilderness and the farm. It somehow held us all, till 1939 – the Second World War broke out and wrought such havoc on this once so glorious and happy home".

The Hall was requisitioned at the outbreak of the Second World War, for use by the King's Liverpool Regiment. The Dowager Countess wrote that *"we had to learn all about passwords and get accustomed to guards and patrols. A cannon was placed on the drive! Every Sunday troops filled the Church at 11 o'clock and afterwards there was a Church Parade – the salute was taken on the front doorstep. It was unbelievably difficult – problems and difficulties were hurled at us. We tried to do battle with them, for the sake of Staunton and all it stood for – truth, love and beauty".*

After six months the family had to move out and they took up residence in the Chaplain's house, which they called the "Parsonage". The Hall became a prison camp for Italian prisoners of war, who did what the Countess described as "hideous damage" to the whole of the property. The Italians were followed by German prisoners, who were hard-working and behaved better and tried to repair some of the damage. When they left

after the war the place lay silent and untended: the heart had stopped beating.

The Hall suffered so greatly that when it was handed back to the family after the War it was in such a state of disrepair that the family was unable to return to it. In addition, there was a threat of open-cast mining on the estate, to ease the post-war fuel crisis. (Before the war, coal cost 19/6d [97.5p] a ton: after the war it cost £8 a ton, which is one reason why the Ferrers family could not afford to heat the Hall to a reasonable temperature).

The Hall as it was left at the end of the Second World War

It is difficult now, in affluent times, to remember how hard our economy and our self-confidence had been knocked by the time the war ended in 1945. There was no money for anything but essentials. Food rationing did not end until 1954. Big old furniture and big old buildings were just not wanted: indeed it was hard to see how they could ever be wanted again without the families and the wealth which once supported them. One by one the big houses were turned over to institutional use or pulled down for the lead on the roofs and other building material. The great rambling hall at Garendon near Loughborough went for brick rubble under the newly built M1 motorway nearby. Others had disappeared much earlier. Those who had known and loved these houses felt saddened but resigned.

In the summer of 1954 the 12th Earl Ferrers finally resigned himself to the inevitable and put his estate up for sale. He had sold some outlying land earlier and agreed with the National Trust to take over the church. The sale was scheduled for 2.30 p.m. on 12th October and the 12th Earl died at 11.30 p.m. the previous evening: no-one doubts that his heart was broken at the thought of his ancestral home being lost to his family. The Countess with her family had to take the difficult decision to let the auction proceed.

No-one was willing to buy the entire estate as one lot and the different properties were offered separately. Even then many lots remained unsold. It was at this time that the walled gardens were purchased by Stan Watson, a nurseryman.

The Hall, together with Melbourne Lodge, gardens and lakes and woodlands totalling 70 acres, was sold to a demolition firm for £14,000. John Blunt's father was at the sale with other local business men, but no-one felt that the price was too low, so much had these houses become "white elephants". It was assumed that the wrecking ball would soon be pulverising the walls of one more stately home.

The Chapel was not sold but was given by the 12th Earl to the National Trust. The Countess said to Mrs Frances ("Sissy") Williams, who lived in a gatehouse very near to the Hall and Chapel: "Please look after my little Chapel for me". This Mrs Williams did faithfully until her death in 1997. Many visitors to the Chapel will recall with affection how Mrs Williams took them round, explained everything to them and even played the organ for them. She was rewarded for her loyalty by the presentation of a National Trust long-service medal on her 90th birthday in 1991.

The 12th Earl may have been devastated by the loss of Staunton Harold. But he had sown a seed which was to lead to a wonderful future for the property and a legacy of which he could be truly proud. He had suffered a serious illness in 1951 and had gone to Cornwall to recuperate. In Cornwall he met Group Captain Leonard Cheshire who took the Earl and his Countess over "St. Teresa's", a home which he had just opened in some nissen huts. The Earl met some of the patients and saw over the Home, including its two chapels, one Church of England and the other Roman Catholic, and was very impressed by all that he saw. His widow later recalled that one evening when they were discussing what could be done with Staunton, he said: "If only Leonard Cheshire could come here – how wonderful that would be not only for us but for the whole of the neighbourhood for miles around".

When the Earl died, the Dowager Countess wrote to Leonard Cheshire and asked whether any of the Earl's clothes would be of use to the residents in his homes. But Leonard Cheshire replied in an unexpected way by asking whether Staunton Harold could become one of his Homes. She described her own feelings: "And then the heavens *did* open. Can you imagine the indescribable thanks and rejoicings?". Cheshire had never seen Staunton Harold but he had read in the newspapers about its sale for demolition – the idea of the destruction of such a property had naturally aroused great opposition from historical and preservation groups and had received national publicity. Leonard Cheshire resolved to try to buy it and "came to the Midlands with very little money in his pocket but with very much faith in his heart, to try to buy this old and lovely house". He said: "If it is God's

The 13th Earl Ferrers.

will that I come, He will lead us, but we must all work together in utter faith. How shall we begin?"

But that is a story which will be told a little later.

Robert the 12th Earl and his Countess Hermione (Morley) had three children, Robert, Penelope and Elizabeth. Robert became the 13th Earl in difficult circumstances but has lived up to the family motto "Honour is the reward of virtue" and enhanced it. He now lives in Ditchingham Hall, a Queen Anne house in Norfolk which belonged to the family of his wife, Annabel (Carr). He served in the Coldstream Guards and took a degree in agriculture at Cambridge University. He farms his estate very efficiently and has also been extremely active on the national scene, describing himself as "a farmer who got caught up in the slip-stream of politics". A member of the Privy Council since 1982, he served as a Minister under five Prime Ministers, from Harold Macmillan to John Major. He held many Government offices, including being Minister of State in the Ministry of Agriculture, the Department of Trade and Industry, the Department of the Environment and in the Home Office, where for over six years he had responsibility for Fire Services and the Police – which made it rather ironic when his house was burgled and the 6ft 5inch Earl set about the intruder with his walking stick! He was Deputy Leader of the House of Lords for the Conservative Governments, and when the hereditary peers had to select 92 of their own number to remain in the House pending its re-organisation by the present Labour Government, Earl Ferrers topped the poll – a clear indication of the respect felt for him by his fellow peers. An active Anglican, he is also High Steward of Norwich Cathedral, as well as holding many other positions in the service of the public. He has five children the eldest of whom, Viscount Tamworth, has gone back to live in the Derbyshire village of Shirley with which the family has been linked for 1000 years.

CHAPTER SEVEN

A FEW TALES AND LEGENDS

*E*very house and family has its own stories and legends. Staunton Harold and the Ferrers family are no exception and some of their tales are worthy of preservation.

THE BULL

Katherine Everett referred to the 10th Earl having to walk around the bull in the entrance hall. The bull had alarmed her on her arrival at the Hall:

"When I got into the stone-flagged hall I was immediately met by the glass-eyed stare of an enormous bull.... The stuffed bull had wide horns and stood on a wooden platform, a perfect toy for giant children, but they would have had to be twenty feet high to have played with him. He was a specimen from the herd, descendants of Roman cattle who roamed the park at Chartley Castle".

Katherine was not the only one to remember this bull. Mrs Margaret Champ started work in Staunton Hall as a trainee scullery maid in 1906, when she was 14 years old. Her memory was of the *"great Ferrers bull – horns for gentlemen to hang their hats on. It was a real great bull – stuffed; and its eyes staring at you; its head turned a little to the left; its tail – the lot! It frightened me the first time I saw it. I thought it was a bull that had*

The Stuffed Bull now standing at Ditchingham Hall.

got in....The house-maids used to push it out onto the lawn when they had to spring-clean".

Katherine may not have been quite right about the origins of these great white cattle. They probably date from pre-Roman times and are therefore from the ancient British stock which formerly roamed throughout the country. There were several herds of these cattle in different parts of Britain at one time, but now the best known is probably that at Chillingham in Northumberland. They are still very wild and are said to kill a calf which has been handled by a human. There was a herd at Chartley which was enclosed in 1248 and some of this herd went to Whipsnade Zoo. The present Earl has some of these

The bull's head carved on the fireplace in the entrance hall at Staunton Harold.

ancient cattle at Ditchingham and has won prizes from the Rare Breeds Survival Trust for them. But he sees them not just as relics of the past – nor indeed merely as links with his own family's past at Chartley: they are treated as a commercial herd which provides good characteristics needed for the improvement of other breeds.

The stuffed bull which stood in the entrance hall at Staunton in Katherine's time is no longer there, but it has been kept by the family and now proudly stands in Ditchingham Hall. The fireplace in the entrance hall at Staunton Hall is decorated with bulls' skulls. This was then a popular architectural feature, known as *bucrania*, but it was probably used at staunton as a reminder of the herd with which the Ferrers have been associated for so long.

THE LION

Reference has already been made to the great "Medicean" lion on top of the Hall at its south-west front of the Hall, which gave its name to the Lion Front, now known as the Lion Court. (Pevsner says that this lion is made of stone, whereas it is actually made of lead, like the figures on the east front, facing the chapel.) Carved on the rump of this lion are the initials and other reminders of some of the German prisoners of war who were housed in the Hall.

There is an old belief that at midnight this lion comes down from the wall and has a drink from the lake. A little girl lived on the estate, where her father and grandfather were employed. She asked her grandfather whether this tale about the lion coming down for a drink was true, as clearly she found it hard to believe. Her grandfather wisely said to her: "My dear, it is perfectly true that when the lion *hears* the clock strike midnight, he comes down for a drink from the lake. But his poor old leaden ears do not hear very well".

Leaden lion overlooking the south front of Staunton Harold Hall, the Lion Front or Lion Court.

THE HORSESHOES

Wherever one looks at Staunton Harold, there are horseshoes. They are to be found painted in the family coat of arms, carved in stone on the gateposts, carved in wood on the fireplace in the Earl's Dining Room, moulded in plaster on the estate buildings and cast in iron as door-handles and knockers.

It is not only at Staunton Harold that horseshoes are a feature of the Ferrers family. The castle at Oakham in Rutland was built in the reign of Henry II by Walchline de Ferrers. All that remains of the castle is the great Hall, now the Magistrates' Court, on whose walls are hung many horseshoes of a vast variety of sizes. Each Peer of the Realm who passed through Oakham was required to pay a tribute to the Lord of the Manor by presenting him with a horseshoe, which was then displayed in the Hall: many of them have crowns on them, and all display the names of the donors, one of the earliest of whom was Queen Elizabeth I.

What is the reason for this Ferrers family pre-occupation with horseshoes?

The origins of the name Ferraris, borne by that Henry to whom the estate was given by William the Conqueror, is not really known. Wain says that it comes from the mining town of La Ferriere-St Hilaire in Normandy and that there is no truth in the legend that the original Ferrers was a master-farrier entrusted with the shoeing of the King's horses. He is probably right about this – a farrier, however able, would not have been given over 200 lordships! But the name of La Ferriere itself, and therefore the name Ferrers, must come from the words in Latin *(ferrum, ferreus)* and/or French *(fer, ferrique, ferreux)* which relate to iron: this would clearly be appropriate for the name of a mining town, just like Ironville close to Staunton. This would explain why horse-shoes are incorporated into the Ferrers family coat of arms, as it has for many years been customary for heraldic devices to include puns on family names.

Head Groom by the stables. The handle on the door in the background is in the shape of a horseshoe.

The horse-shoes on Dorothy Watson's house at Staunton Harold

But this rather prosaic explanation for the proliferation of horse-shoes at Staunton is far less romantic than the explanation offered by Katherine Everett. She was told that the horseshoes, which she first noticed on the footman's uniform, were *"in memory of the escape of Mary Queen of Scots from Chartley Castle, when she rode away on a horse shod with horse-shoes mounted on three stilts to disguise the manner of her going"*. Whether it is true or not, that is a story which many people like to believe about the Ferrers' horse-shoes!

THE RED HAND

It has already been noted in connection with the family crest in the chapel that the Baronet's crest incorporates the Red Hand of Ulster, which itself is derived from the legend about the way in which the Earldom of Ulster was claimed by the O'Neills. This story has already been told in connection with the crest on the organ in the Chapel. (see page 20)

Like many other families which have Baronetcies, the Shirleys have often had to explain away other more sanguinary reasons given for this Red Hand being in their coat of arms. Wain records one of these stories from Staunton, that the "bloody hand" could be removed from the coat of arms only if someone could be found who would renounce the world and live as a hermit or anchorite for a specified number of years. He also says that there is another story, that one finger of the Hand was wiped out on the accession of each successive holder of the title.

But the historic reason for the Hand is well documented, even if its origins may be mythical.

THE SARACEN'S HEAD

Like most noble families of their period, members of the Staunton and Shirley families went on the Crusades during the Middle Ages. It was often the wish of the family that this form of service should not be forgotten, and a Saracen's head was illustrated somewhere as a reminder.

At Staunton Harold there is the Saracen's Head in the Chapel as a permanent reminder of the family's service in the Crusades. But there is also the nearby Saracen's Head pub at Heath End, whose connections with the Crusades are more difficult to justify, though the name comes from the pub's connections with the Shirley/Ferrers family and the Staunton Harold estate. This pub was rebuilt in its present position by the 10th Earl: formerly it stood in the fields besides the drive and was called the Elm Tree Inn.

CHAPTER EIGHT

STAUNTON HAROLD AS A CHESHIRE HOME

We have seen how Group Captain Leonard Cheshire V.C., D.S.C., D.F.C. came to the East Midlands to try to secure Staunton Harold for use as a home for the war-wounded and other people with disabilities for whom he had perceived a great need. No-one wanted to see the Hall demolished and a Preservation Order had been put on it for 6 months after the initial sale, to see whether an alternative use could be found for it. Leonard Cheshire was perhaps the only person who thought that something really could and should be done to save the Hall. He came to Staunton and agreed to buy it – not that there was any money to buy it with, but after so many years of flying "on a wing and a prayer" maybe he viewed things differently from most people. The demolition firm wanted £16,500 to resell the Hall to him. It was a near run thing but a few days before completion was due a city financier advanced £10,000 as a interest-free loan and a public appeal produced the balance needed.

When a bold man shows the way others will follow. It was amazing how much enthusiastic help was instantly forthcoming to help turn the old place round. Nearly all the work of mending the roofs, repairing, cleaning and decorating was done by volunteers. Cash was desperately short.

Russell Brandon, in his biography "Cheshire VC", gives a dramatic account of what happened:

"This ancestral home, called Staunton Harold, was in such a state of dilapidation that not only had it already been sold for demolition but also, by the winter of 1955, it had become irresistible to Cheshire.

"Here, where snow melted on the ancient roofs and trickled continuously and horribly through gaping holes in the masonry and ran all the way down to the freezing stone floors of the great hall; where all was desolation and decay; where the wrecker's bull-dozers waited impatiently to nudge and pulverise the lot – here was the perfect site, Leonard considered, for a home. But to get it back he had to find £16,000. So he found it!

"Promptly Leicestershire and the Midlands went berserk with buckets and scrubbing brushes, pipes and sluices for plumbing, wire for electrical re-wiring, paint, furniture and week-end working parties. In a surprisingly short time, Staunton Harold became habitable, patients moved in and a staff was found to look after them. The Historic Buildings Council – which only a few months previously had been quite content to let bull-dozers pound the mansion into oblivion – were now so astounded by the transformation wrought that they produced a large grant. With this the magnificent old house was fully restored; and Cheshire's fifth home, its beginnings as improbable as those of each of the other four, became in 1955 a flourishing fact".

John Blunt was one of the local people involved at that time. He recalls how, when he was on leave from the army, he was set to work smashing out fireplaces to sell as scrap iron. He took out stoves which the army had left – but also Georgian fireplaces whose removal would have been unacceptable and illegal today. But as he says: *"We were achieving two objectives at once, providing a home for up to 40 people and rescuing a magnificent house".*

The Dowager Countess Ferrers was thrilled about the new use for the home in which she and her family had been so happy. When she heard that Leonard

Cheshire wanted Staunton to be used as one of his Foundation Homes, she wrote: *"Can you imagine the indescribable thanks and rejoicings? The news that Staunton Harold was to become a Cheshire Home spread like wild-fire and was immediately followed by the most staggering offers of help…. The work was filthy and frightful but it was all done in happiness….One Sunday there were 85 people at work in the house and 30 in the garden…All gave their time and their talents"*.

The 12th Earl's dream had come true, despite his disappointment at the need to sell the Hall.

In June 1955 the first residents moved in. Some of them were there for many years and became active members of the community and good friends of local people. Under a succession of dedicated wardens, often ex-forces personnel, the Cheshire Home prospered.

Support groups were formed in a dozen nearby towns and villages, the *Friends of Staunton*.

One big fund-raiser which the *Friends* started was the annual fete, usually held on the first Saturday in September. This grew until it attracted crowds of 7000 or 8000 people each year: it marked the beginning of large-scale visitor numbers at Staunton

It seemed as if everyone was willing to help not only to save Staunton but also to help those who were being helped by Leonard Cheshire. The Dowager Countess gave great help and encouragement to the venture and wrote to a friend: *"A miracle has happened and my beloved Staunton is going to be saved"*. Courtaulds provided curtains for the windows and firms as far away as Blackburn & Starling, the engineering company in Kirk White St in Nottingham encouraged their staff to help at Staunton and to support its

The opening of Staunton Harold Hall as a Cheshire Home. Arthur Crane, Chairman of the Management Committee, is standing. The 13th Earl Ferrers and Group Captain Cheshire are seated in the centre of the picture.

fund-raising events. The Matron said: *"People have a way of turning up from outside when they are needed. That is part of the miracle of Staunton"*.

In 1955, on one of his frequent visits to Staunton, Leonard Cheshire received gifts for the Home which were typical – £65 from Castle Donington and District Cage Bird Society, £21-15-6d (£21.77p) from the National Federation of Business and Professional Women's Clubs. There were displays and a barbecue to raise more money. The Group Captain said: *"Staunton is one of the strongest homes we have got, and there has never been such a volume of support as there is here"*.

The Cheshire Home at Staunton was well-equipped and functional, but much of the old family feeling was retained. A lift was installed – but the staircase was restored as a wonderful example of the craftsman's skill. Bedrooms had become wards, but still retained names such as The Lake Room, Earl Ferrer's Room. The library was restored to its designed purpose and Ferrers family portraits hung in the Earl's Dining Room.

Russell Brandon said of Leonard Cheshire: *"By now Cheshire had learned what it was to take others some considerable time to learn – that his great gift to the incurably ill of Britain lay not in nursing them, not even in running homes for them, but in starting homes for them and then, leaving their running to a committee, moving off to start another home somewhere else"*. This is certainly what he did, very successfully, at Staunton Harold.

A Cheshire Home has been described as "a place of shelter physically, and of encouragement spiritually; a place in which the residents can acquire a sense of belonging and of ownership by contributing in any way within their capabilities to its functioning and development; a place to share with others, and from which to help others less fortunate; a place in which to gain confidence and develop independence and interests; a place of hopeful endeavour and not of passive disinterest".

The residents at Staunton Harold did not sit back and take advantage of the efforts of other people. Not only did they enhance their wonderful surroundings by their own efforts, they also contributed to the joy which filled Staunton again. The poem reproduced at the beginning of this booklet sums up their feelings well. But Tom Gair, who wrote that poem, inspired patients, staff and the wider community in a variety of ways. A spastic from birth, Tom went to Staunton in 1957. In 1959 he wrote the script for a pantomime "Cinders of Staunton Hall" which was a triumph. Patients endured and overcame their discomforts for the sake of the pantomime, which gave enormous pleasure not only to the patients themselves but also to many others. Typical of the brave performers was George Barnes (Buttons) who was both blind and crippled and had to learn his part through people continually repeating it to him. The miracle of the buildings was continued among the patients, who took a new lease of life by being part of such a marvellous community.

Those fortunate to be given the opportunity to live in the Cheshire Home at Staunton Harold certainly lived up to the founder's intention that they should contribute to their home, develop interests and independence, and acquire a sense of belonging. There were fetes and car rallies, concerts and countless other fund-raising events at Staunton.

Leonard Cheshire took a personal interest in all of these activities, and visited Staunton on many occasions. Sue Ryder wrote in her autobiography "Child of my love": *"..we met at intervals at Staunton Harold…on brief visits to help restore this large and lovely house"*. Leonard Cheshire married Sue Ryder, who was herself already well known for her work on behalf of Nazi concentration camp victims.

Staunton Harold was a Cheshire Home for the physically handicapped from 1955 to 1985. It was not ideal for the purpose as the residents, though physically handicapped, were not normally bed-bound, but the nature of the building limited their ability to move around freely. In 1985 the work was therefore moved into single-story premises 15 miles away at Newlands House, Netherseal, near Measham in Derbyshire, with some of the residents moving to the Cheshire Home in Lady Bay, Nottinghamshire. At both of these Cheshire Homes excellent care continues to be provided for the disabled residents. When the Cheshire Home moved to Netherseal, Staunton Harold was "kept in the family", as it was sold to the Ryder Cheshire Mission.

Sue Ryder and Leonard Cheshire had been looking around the Midlands for some years to try to find somewhere suitable to be the Headquarters of their

Leonard Cheshire and Sue Ryder. (Picture by kind permission of the Reader's Digest)

joint Mission. The future of Staunton Harold had looked uncertain again when the Cheshire Home moved out, but now an appropriate new purpose had been found and Staunton Harold became the base for the Ryder Cheshire Mission.

When he visited Staunton Harold in 1987 in connection with the new venture, Leonard Cheshire said: *"I think the people of Staunton Harold are wonderful. I have also been overwhelmed by the concern they have shown to their fellow human beings who are less fortunate than themselves, and for the Hall itself. It feels great to be back home"*.

The Ryder Cheshire Mission was founded in 1959 to undertake projects which met a clear need but did not fall within the scope of either the Leonard Cheshire or the Sue Ryder Foundation. The Ryder Cheshire Mission is active in many countries including Australia, India, Italy, Nepal, New Zealand and Tanzania. The Mission provides for people with a variety of needs including

- those whose leprosy has been cured.
- severely mentally handicapped children.
- those who are blind or have other disabilities.
- refugees.
- cancer out-patients.

Training and rehabilitation are provided for many residents.

So Staunton Harold became the Headquarters of the Ryder Cheshire Mission. Most of the Hall was leased from the Mission to provide accommodation for the Sue Ryder Care Home. But the Hall also housed not only the administration of the Mission but also a project to collect information about the needs of people with handicaps who live in villages in the Third World, a museum and a display designed to illustrate the special problems faced everywhere by people with disabilities. The Leonard Cheshire Archives were also kept at Staunton Harold.

Another change took place at the end of 1999. The Ryder Cheshire Mission moved to Bristol and the accommodation which was released at Staunton Harold became the national headquarters of the Heath-care service of Sue Ryder Care, with responsibility for overseeing the quality of services delivered in all the Sue Ryder Homes in the United Kingdom and providing for the expansion of services when that is needed. Thus Staunton Harold continued to provide a base from which good works spread throughout the land.

However in 2001 the Ryder Cheshire Mission decided that it must sell Staunton Harold in order to release funds for its work elsewhere and the future of the Hall therefore became uncertain again.

CHAPTER NINE

SUE RYDER CARE AT STAUNTON HAROLD

Staunton Harold Hall became a Sue Ryder Home in 1989, the premises being leased from the Ryder-Cheshire Mission. It was one of 20 Sue Ryder Care Centres in Britain and one of 7 specialising in palliative care, which is the active total care of patients whose disease cannot be cured. Importantly, Staunton Harold did not restrict its services for patients with particular diagnoses. This meant that patients cared for at the Home were assessed according to their needs and may have had a variety of medical conditions, unlike other hospices. None were excluded on the basis of their diagnosis.

Care at Staunton Harold concentrated on meeting patients' needs, which is sometimes referred to as holistic care. This may involve controlling pain and other symptoms, physical, psychological and spiritual support. There was a full team of staff working together to help patients and, as importantly, their families or carers. The team included highly trained and experienced doctors, nurses, social workers, occupational therapists and a chaplain. The services included in-patient care, usually for around 14 days, or attendance at Day Care once a week. Both services were available for palliative care, including respite for family/carers. Staunton Harold was a happy place with staff who were dedicated to providing good quality patient care. There was always a family atmosphere at Staunton Harold Hall, although it was no longer the Ferrers' family home.

The care team at Staunton Harold was much wider than those providing direct patient care. Numerous

Sue Ryder Day Care patients enjoying activities at Staunton Harold.

other members of staff were integral to the successful running of the Centre, including administration, domestic, catering, gardening, maintenance and security staff. In several areas paid staff were assisted by a team of hard-working and enthusiastic volunteers. A dedicated fund-raising unit completed the overall team at Staunton, striving endlessly to ensure that services could be maintained, developed and improved, taking care into the 21st century.

Financially the Centre was also supported by Sue Ryder Care nationally. But the bulk of the income the Centre received to support came from the surrounding five Health Authorities. This last source of funding was radically affected by changes in the National Health Service and the establishment of local Primary Care Trusts (P.C.T.). When the P.C.T. first in Derbyshire and then in Leicestershire decided to send fewer if any patients to Staunton Harold, it appeared that the Centre could not be maintained for the small number of patients who came from other areas. As this change coincided with the decision of the Ryder-Cheshire Mission to sell the Hall to release funds to be used elsewhere to carry out the Mission's functions, the closure of the Sue Ryder Care Centre at Staunton Harold began to look probable at the end of 2001.

Closure would mean the end of the caring work carried out at Staunton Harold for nearly half a century first by Leonard Cheshire's foundation and then by the organisation set up by his wife. But the work of the Leonard Cheshire Foundation and of Sue Ryder Care will continue in other parts of Britain and indeed throughout the world.

Leonard Cheshire and Sue Ryder loved Staunton Harold and worked together there. The work done at Staunton Harold in the 20th century by the Foundations which they established will never be forgotten.

At a meeting of volunteers held on 11th September 2001 two documents were circulated.

The Ryder Cheshire Foundation issued a statement which, after retracing the history of the foundation's involvement at Staunton Harold (see chapter 8), goes on to say:

> "Ryder Cheshire currently leases the building to Sue Ryder Care for use as a hospice, but does not receive any income from the lease of the Hall. Sue Ryder Care and Ryder Cheshire held discussions earlier in the year about the future of Staunton Harold Hall at which Ryder Cheshire indicated that it would like to sell the Hall and realise the asset."

Sue Ryder Care at Staunton Harold issued an update in which Julie Smith, Sue Ryder Care Director of Healthcare and Nursing, said:

> "Had it not been for the disposal of the property, Leicestershire Health Authority, North West Leicestershire Primary Care Group and Greater Derby Primary Care Trust have confirmed that they would have continued to commission Sue Ryder Care for the provision of care at Staunton Harold... In view of the pressure placed on us by Ryder Cheshire to vacate Staunton Harold Hall we are investigating the future viability of many different options for the provision of palliative care for local people and at this stage nothing is being discounted. In the meantime we are committed to the care of our patients both present and future, and of course to our staff."

At the time of going to press, nothing is known about the future of Sue Ryder Care at Staunton Harold, or of the Hall itself, beyond what was said in these two statements.

CHAPTER TEN

ADAPTING TO CHANGE
Staunton Harold Over the Last 50 Years

by JOHN BLUNT

*F*ifty years ago you had to have a reason to go down the long drives to the little community at Staunton Harold, rather as you would to go down a private drive today. It was especially tantalizing because this beautiful place was visible down in the valley, basking in the morning sun, as you drove along the Melbourne to Ashby road. We locals knew that most of the buildings we could see stood empty and decaying, which only added to the air of mystery.

My family were lucky to have a reason to visit the Home Farm behind the Hall occasionally. We went to buy cattle for our butchery business at Melbourne. One of my early memories is of watching surveyors at work near the Hall. They were exploring the feasibility of demolishing part of

The Gamekeeper's cottage on the Staunton Harold Estate, now demolished.

the building to make it compact enough for the 12th Earl and his family to move back into it. Nothing came of it. One of the remarkable things about Staunton Harold is that so little of importance has been built or demolished at Staunton over the last 100 years. Before the estate sale the River Dove Water Board had purchased a swathe of land at the northern end of the park for their new reservoir and demolished some

cottages and the gamekeeper's house which Katherine Everett wrote about. Statutory authorities are often not very good custodians of old buildings.

The Staunton Harold estate was offered for sale by auction in 1954. Not many lots found a buyer on the day and sales by private treaty dragged on into the following year. The three farms which make up the core of the estate were bought by my father in 1955. They were all tenanted farms and in reasonable repair. It was otherwise with the stable block, at the rear of the Hall, which was "thrown in" with the Home Farm as having very little value. This enormous building had been at the heart of the working estate. There was stabling for 40 horses, two carriage houses, a dovecote, two granaries, a blacksmith's shop and accommodation for a great many staff.

When I first knew the place it had stood shut up and abandoned for many years. Trees had grown up by the walls and their branches had swept great swathes of slates off the roof. The courtyard was knee-high in grass and weeds. The rooms were mostly empty, the stalls and mangers still in place just as the last horse had left them. We set to work to make the roofs watertight and then cast around to find a use for it.

The process took us 20 years. At various times we tried unsuccessfully to obtain permission for conversion to houses and for bulk storage so when in 1974 Geoff Herbert came asking if he could rent some rooms to start a pottery, I sent him off to the Council offices without much expectation of seeing him again. To my surprise he was back a few weeks later. "I've got my permission, now where can I start?" We let him the space he needed at 10 shillings (50p) per week.

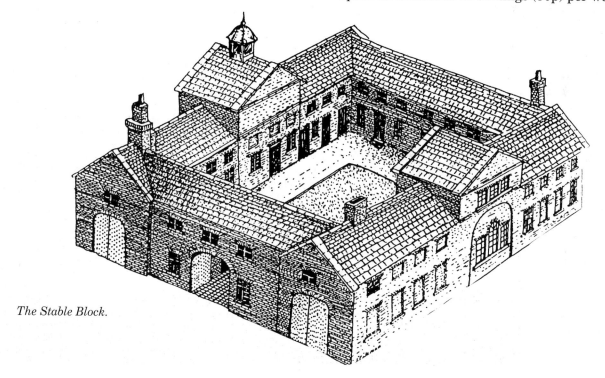

The Stable Block.

Shortly afterwards the whole stableblock was "listed" Grade II with all the requirements to keep it in good repair. I sought a meeting with the planners and asked them what use they would allow the buildings to be put to. They replied that they would favour craft workshops and accommodation for craftspeople. It was a relief to have some direction to head for at last.

We already had the potter and the next thing was to make a house for him. Then partly through advertisements but mainly by word of mouth we began to let other workshops. The newly emerging interest in crafts at the time led to craft fairs and when these became overpriced a number of people approached us for permanent workshops. The rent was important but the quality of the work was mixed so in 1985 my wife Jackie and I took a hard look at where we wanted the Centre to go. We decided to aim for quality and the highest possible standards. It meant leaving workshops empty sometimes but it seems to have paid off: other centres have come and gone but we are busier than we have ever been, with more craftspeople working under one roof than any other venue I know in Britain. Since our emphasis is on contemporary craftsmanship we also changed our name to *The Ferrers Centre for Arts and Crafts.*

In 1991 we converted one of the granaries into the *Ferrers Gallery,* to display and sell the work of craftspeople from all over Britain. This has expanded to take up three floors showing the work of several hundred makers. Contemporary furniture and woodwork is displayed along with ironwork, ceramics, jewellery, textiles and glass.

The former stable block courtyard is now the focal point of the Ferrers Centre for Arts and Crafts.

Bringing the public in, first to the Hall, then to the Nurseries and finally to the *Ferrers Centre* has had a big impact on Staunton Harold. Sometimes, especially at Bank Holidays, people who live at Staunton complain at "the public" descending on them in such numbers. It can be annoying, especially when residents cannot get out of their own front drives, but I tend to remind them and myself that it was these visitors who ultimately saved the splendid group of buildings which make up Staunton Harold today. If no-one came, some of us would be struggling again. The fact is, we need visitors – but not too many!

Traffic is a particular problem. There are three miles of internal roads to maintain. In 1992 a committee was formed to co-ordinate traffic and parking issues. In 1997 a one-way traffic system was introduced so that the road verges would not be churned up by vehicles constantly passing each other. Because of divided ownership it is not practicable to charge for parking: voluntary collections on Bank

Holidays have largely funded road repairs in recent years. As I write this in 2001 we estimate our visitor numbers at about 175,000 per year. Our aim is to accommodate the vehicles which bring these large numbers without losing the intimate feeling of a rural estate.

The landscape at Staunton is very adequately protected: Conservation Area status, Tree Preservation Orders, National Trust covenants – can we have too much of a good thing, I sometimes wonder? These are negative measures, they stop owners doing things without motivating them to do something good. Ultimately it is up to the various owners to maintain and enhance what they own. Nature does not stand still: trees need pruning, thinning and replanting, lakes need dredging and weirs have to be rebuilt. For my part I love the work: no day is better spent than in doing work at Staunton. It is a good place to be at any time – but come the evening, when the crowds have gone, I look across the valley and agree with Pevsner, it is a very special piece of England.

The social order has changed enormously since

Stud Groom on the estate early in the 20th century.

the time of the 10th Earl. 100 years ago Staunton was a self-contained community working under the direction of one man in a hierarchy of prestige and privilege. Today the buildings and landscape are owned by a dozen different families and visited by tens of thousands. The numbers who live and work here are probably not much changed but now they are independent of each other. That they do not all pull in opposite ways suggests to me that they have fallen under the spell of Staunton. Are they as happy? Yes, I think they are. The State has replaced the Earl as the "cradle to grave" provider. Instead of the caprices of one man we now endure the endless interference of government.

I am a traditionalist at heart. While harbouring no illusions about the drawbacks of the "good old days", I

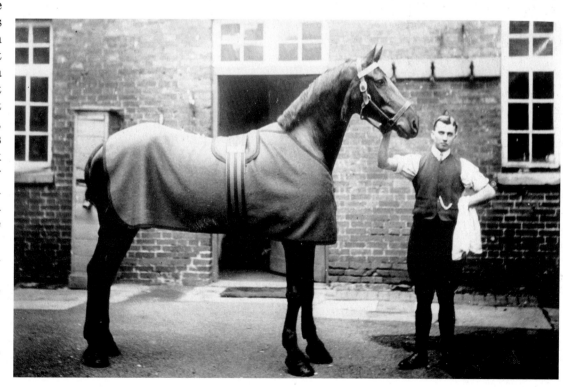

Mr Shaw, Woodman, with his axe, the symbol of his trade. The present Head Woodman on the Staunton Harold Estate is a descendant of Mr Shaw.

regret the fact that we seldom do things for ourselves today "in house" in the modern parlance. As a boy I loved to stand watching at the forge of Harry Roberts, our Melbourne blacksmith. Harry had learned his trade with his father at Breedon on the Hill, two miles from Staunton Harold. The Staunton forge was seldom used and every few months Harry would be sent over on foot to collect and return such items as needed the blacksmith's attention. He would collect axes for sharpening from the woodsmen, hoes and spades from the gardeners, items from the stables and from the big house. The steward would send him to the brewery, which is a separate building behind the Hall, for a pint or two of home-brewed ale. He must have needed it with all that weight to carry back to Breedon. Lastly, on his way home, he would call in on the gamekeeper at his house below the bottom dam, where maybe he would be given a brace of rabbits. All this Harry would tell me as he drew hot iron from the forge and the sparks were flying.

Well, we have not restarted the brewery yet but we have rekindled an unusual amount of self-sufficiency. Staunton has a blacksmith again in the original forge, and also woodsmen and joiners, gardeners, builders and stonemasons. The trees from the woods go once again to our own sawmill and joiner's shop. Some of the wood is used by the furniture makers at the *Ferrers Centre*. When we need doors or windows or beams or fencing stakes we cut them from our own timber in the time-honoured way. The waste wood goes to fire the kilns for our potter or to heat the stoves in other workshops. And as we fell, so we replant. The Staunton Estate has grown again these last 50 years and now includes 400 acres of woodland. Every year we are planting trees in the larger woods, replacing lost spinneys and individual parkland trees. The rewards are more than aesthetic: a local ornithologist records his sightings on the estate and each year his list grows steadily longer.

I suppose all of this betrays my own particular passion, which is for the woods and the trees. As it happens I have never hunted, shot or fished, though I am more than happy for these activities to continue at Staunton. It may be a consequence of this that we are more relaxed about public access than some other rural estates. Over the last seven years we have made four miles of new footpaths and bridleways through the woods and farmland. They are immensely popular and have not been abused.

So the landscape at Staunton enters the 21st century in good heart although farming is going through bad times again and countryside issues are hotly debated. We will need to be nimble to stay ahead. Whatever befalls the Hall, it will not be pulled down: the beauty of Staunton is secure and accessible to all. I hope you enjoy it as I do, and will come back many times.

STAUNTON HAROLD: A SELECT BIBLIOGRAPHY

BECKETT, J.V.: *Northamptonshire Past and Present*. VIII, 1993/4. "The sale of Astwell and Falcutt in 1774-78".

BRANDON R: *Cheshire V.C.* Evans, 1965

CANTOR, Leonard: *The Historic Country Houses of Leicesterhire and Rutland*. Kairos Press 1998

COUNTRY LIFE: 5th   April 1913; 12th   April 1913; 10th   May 1979; 27th   September 1962

CRANE. A: *The Kirkland Papers 1753 – 1869.* Crane Press 1990

DERBYSHIRE LIFE AND COUNTRYSIDE. March 1967.

DRIVE PUBLICATIONS: *Treasures of Britain*. 1968

DORNIER, Ann: *Mercian Studies*. Leicester University Press 1977

EVERETT K: *Bricks and Flowers*. The Reprint Society 1951.

GAIR, T.: *Sitting in his invalid's chair sets down in rhyme a few of his thoughts.*

GENTRY P.W.: *The Countess of Huntingdon*. Foundery Press

KIRBY G.W.: *The Elect Lady*. Countess of Huntingdon's Connexion 1990

LACEY A.C.: Sir Robert Shirley and the English Revolution in Leicestershire.
    Leicestershire Archaeological and Historical Society Transactions. Vol. LVIII 1982/3

LANE M.: *The Queen of Methodists*. City of Worcester Building Preservation Trust 1987

NICHOLS, J.: *The History and Antiquities of the County of Leicester*. 1804.

OSMAN L.: *Staunton Harold Leicestershire & Foremark, Derbyshire. Two Laudian churches now under
    restoration*. Ancient Monuments Society 1956.

PEVSNER N.: *The Buildings of England – Leicestershire*. Penguin 1960

PEVSNER N.: *The Buildings of England – Warwickshire*. Penguin 1966

PROGRAMME of the TERCENTENARY CELEBRATIONS in the Chapel at Staunton Harold.
    26th September 1953.

SIMMONS J. & COLVIN H.M.: Staunton Harold Chapel. *Archaeological Journal* CXII 1955.

STARKEY, Drucella: *The Cheshire Home at Staunton Harold*. 1967

STENTON D.M.: *English Society in the Early Middle Ages*. Pelican 1952.

THE NATIONAL TRUST: *Staunton Harold Church*. 1999

THE TIMES : 15th April 1953

Various publications from the Sue Ryder Care Foundation, newspaper cuttings and local leaflets relating to
    Staunton Harold.

WAIN H. J.: *The Story of Staunton Harold*. W.E.A. 1965

WALTER, 11th EARL FERRERS on behalf of Rev. Roland Borough. "The Chapel at Staunton Harold".
    Proceedings of the Society of Antiquaries. 12th March 1914

WILLIAMS B.C.J: *The Story of St Mary and St Hardulph Church, Breedon on the Hill.*

WOOD R.O.: "Reverend Theophilus Henry Hastings". *The Leake Historian*. Winter 1994/5

Sincere thanks are also due to Mrs Dorothy Watson for all her help and encouragement, Mrs Margaret Crossley of the Countess of Huntingdon's Connexion, Leicestershire County Archives, Libraries and Museums Services, the Leonard Cheshire Foundation and to innumerable individuals whose contributions and reminiscences have given this booklet an individual and local flavour. Any faults which remain are the responsibility of the author and not of those who have given him so much help and made his task such a pleasure.

INDEX

A

Agincourt, Battle of: 11
Arts and Crafts, Ferrers Centre for: 39, 44, **65**, **66**
Ashby de la Zouch: 25, 27
Ashby Lodge: **40**

B

Baddesley Clinton: 9
Bailey, Miss: **45**
Bakewell, Robert: 20, 32
Barnes, George: 59
Baronets, order of: 14
Betjeman, John: 22
Blunt, John: 36, 42, 44, 48, 51, 57, 64
Brandon, Russell: 57, 59
Breedon on the Hill: **10**, 13, 29, 31
Breedon Priory: 13
bull, stuffed: 46, **53** - **54**
bull's head carving: **54**
Burton-on-Trent: 44
Byron, Lord: 29

C

Calke Abbey: 15, 48
Calke Mill: 41, 44
Campbell, Lord Frederick: 29
Castle Donington: 15
Champ, Mrs Margaret: 53
Chapel of the Holy Trinity: **8**, 15 - 22, 39, 49, 56
　altar silver: **21**
　box pews: 20
　ceiling: 19
　clock, diagonal: 22
　inscription: 18, 22
　interior: **19**
　organ: 20
　screen: 20
Charles II: 23 - 24
Chartley Castle: **11**, 12, 16, 56, 63
Cheshire Home: 5, 39, 48, 59 - 60
Cheshire, Leonard: 31, 39, 51 - 52, 57, **58** - **60**, 61, 63
Chichester, Lady Augusta Annabella: 45
Chillingham: 53
Church Pool: 44

Civil War: 15, 22
Clifford, Margaret: 27
Clowne, Walter of Melbourne: 40
coal: 43
Coldstream Guards: 52
Conservative Party: 52
copper mining: 43
Countess of Huntingdon's Connexion: 26
Courtaulds: 58
Crane, Arthur: **58**
Crewe Estate: 44
Cromwell, Oliver: 15, 25
Crusades: 56

D

deer: 41, 48
Derbyshire coalfields: 43
Devereux, Dorothy: 15, 24
Devereux, Robert, Earl of Essex: 12, 15
Dimminsdale: 44
Ditchingham Hall: 52, 54
Donington Hall: 25

E

East Stoke, Battle of: 11
Elm Tree Inn: 56
Essex, Robert Devereux, Earl of: 12, 15
Ettington, Warks: 9, 24 - 25
Everett, Katherine: **46** - **47**, 53, 56, 65

F

family crest: 4, 20, 30
family tree: 30
Ferraris: 55
Ferraris, Henry de: 9
Ferraris, Robert: 9 - 10
Ferrers Centre for Arts and Crafts: 39, 44, **65**, **66**
Ferrers, Dowager Countess: 48, 50 - 52, 57 - 58
Ferrers Gallery: 66
Ferrers, Earl and Viscount Tamworth
　1st Earl, Robert: 24, 32, 36
　2nd Earl, Washington: 25
　4th Earl, Laurence: 26, **27** - 29, 31, 35
　5th Earl, Washington: 25, 31, 33, 35 - 36, 41, 45

6th Earl, Robert: 45
7th Earl, Robert: 45
8thEarl, Washington: 45
9th Earl, Washington Sewalis: 45
10th Earl, Sewallis: 22, 36 - **37**, 39, 42, 45, 47 - 48, 56, 67
11th Earl, Walter: 48 - 49
12th Earl, Robert: 21, 43, **49**, 51 - 52, 58, 64
13th Earl, Robert: **13**, 44, **52**, **58**
Finch, Selina: 24 - 25
Fisher, Geoffrey: 22

G

Gair, Tom: 7, 59
Gamekeeper : **42**, 64
George III: 26, 33
German prisoners of war: 50, 54
Gibbons, Nurse: **38**
Golden Gates : 32, 34
Great Park: 40
Greatbach, Samuel: **42**
Groom: **55**, **67**

H

hanging of 4th Earl Ferrers: **28**
Hardulph, St.: 10, 13
Harold de Lecha: 9
Harpur family: 15
Hastings family: 15
Henderson, William: 35
Henry VIII: 13, 25, 31
Home Farm: 46
horseshoes: 38, 55 - 56
House of Lords: 52
housekeeper: **45**, 46
housemaid: **38**
Huntingdon, Selina, Countess of: 25 - **26**, 28, 41
Huntingdon, Theophilus, Earl of: 25

I

iron: 43
Italian prisoners of war: 38, 50

J

James I: 13
Johnson, John: 27, 29, 38
Jones, Inigo: 36

K

Kirkland, Dr Thomas: 27 - 28
Knight, Walter: 48
Kyrk, Zachary and Samuel: 19

L

Lady Bay, Nottinghamshire: 60
Laud, William: 15, 20 - 21
lead mining: 43
Leake, East and West: 9, 26
Leicester Museum: 21
Leonard Cheshire Foundation: 44, 63
lime quarrying: 43
Lion Front or Lion Court: 33, 35, 37, 54
lion, leaden: **54**
Little Gidding community: 20

M

Melbourne: 44
Melbourne Hall: 20
Melbourne Lodge: 41
Meredith, Mary: 27, 29
Methodist Conference: 25
Midland Railway Company: 44
Moore, John Francis: 25

N

National Trust: 17 - 18, 21, 34, 44, 51
Newlands House, Netherseal: 5, 60
Nichols, John: 31, 35
Nuneaton: 44

O

organ in the chapel: 19, 20

P

Pedigree, Great: 13 - 14
Pedigree, Lesser: 14
pews in the chapel: 20
Plantation of Ulster: 13
Potter, Dr John: 26
prisoners of war: 50, 54

R

Red Hand of Ulster: 13, 20, 56
Royalists: 15
Ryder, Lady Sue: 31, 59 - **60**, 63
Ryder-Cheshire Mission : 6, 61

S

Saracen's head: 21, 56

screen in the chapel: 19
Sealed Knot: 15
Selina: see Huntingdon, Countess of
Shaw, Tom: 37,
Shaw, Mr. (woodman): **68**
Sheldon, Rev. Gilbert: 17, 22
Shepheard, Richard: 19
Shirley arms: 4, 30
Shirley, Baronets
    1st Baronet, Sir George: **12** - 14, 31, 40
    2nd Baronet, Sir Henry: 14 -15, 31, 40
    3rd Baronet, Sir Charles: 15
    4th Baronet Sir Robert: **15**, 17 - 18,
        21 - 22, 32
    5th Baronet, Sir Robert: 42
Shirley Earl Ferrers: see Ferrers
Shirley family crest: 4, 20, 30
Shirley family motto: 36, 52
Shirley family tree (simplified): 30
Shirley, Francis: 13, 31, 40
Shirley, Fulcher: 9
Shirley, Hugh: 11
Shirley, John: 12
Shirley, Lady Katherine: 23
Shirley, Ralph: 11 - 12
Shirley, Rev. Walter: 26, 28, 48
Shirley, Robert, Baron Ferrers of Chartley: 24
Shirley, Saswalo: 9
Shirley, Sir Thomas: 11
Shrewsbury, Battle of: 11
Smith, Mrs: **41**
Smith, William: 19
Spring Wood: 41
St Pancras' Church: 29
Starkey, Mrs Drucella: 48
Staunton Harold Hall **8**, 31-39, **50**
    brewhouse: 38
    central courtyard: **32**
    Chapel: 32
    dairy: 38
    den: 36
    Earl's dining room: 36, **37**, 38, 55, 59
    entrance hall: 36
    gardens: 33
    Ghost Suite: 38
    Golden Gates: 32, **34**
    grand front: **35**
    grand staircase: **24**, 37, 59
    justice room: 31 - **32**

    kitchen: 38
    lamp corridor: **37**
    library: 32, 36
    library front: 36
    lion front or lion court: 33, 35, 37, 54
    parkland: **33**, **43**
    parlour: 36, 38
    private chapel: 31
    saloon: 38, **39**
    servants' hall: 38
Staunton Harold Reservoir: 44
Staunton, Elias: 10
Staunton, Margaret: 12
Sue Ryder Care: 5, 6, 31, 36, 38, 39, 61 - 63
Sue Ryder Day Care Centre: 39, **62**
Swadlincote: 44

T

Ticknall tramway: 43 - 44

U

Ulster, Plantation of: 13, 20, 56
Ulster, Red Hand of : 20, 56

V

Victoria and Albert Museum: 21

W

Wain, H.J.: 5, 41 - 43, 48, 55 - 56
Washington, Elizabeth: 24
Watson, Dorothy: 5, 56
Watson, Job: 37
Watson, Stanley and Dorothy: 5, 44, 51
Wesley, John and Charles: 25 - 26
White, Ina Maud: 45
Wilderness Wood: 44
William III and Queen Anne: 24
William the Conqueror: 9, 55
Williams, Mrs Frances (Sissy): 51
World War I: 48
World War II: 50
woodman: **68**

Y

Yates, Benjamin: 37

(Numbers in bold denote illustrations)